Praise for *Prove It*

"Learning how to build customer trust is essential for small business success, and this book is the perfect 'how to' guide!"
MELINDA EMERSON, "SmallBizLady"; author, *Become Your Own Boss in 12 Months*

"Marketers spend so much time marketing when they should be earning trust. *Prove It* shows you exactly how to do that. No fluff. No wasted space."
RAMON RAY, founder, SmartHustle.com

"Praise be to every deity ever named, we finally have a book that recognizes what content marketing is actually for: trust. Everything else flows from that. Which means everything else flows from this book."
JAY ACUNZO, author, *Break the Wheel*; former marketer, Google, HubSpot, and ESPN

"Melanie Deziel is someone I've watched and respected for years, and this book is just further evidence of her complete mastery over the content marketing space. I'd consider this a must-read for anyone looking to earn the trust of their audience."
KALEIGH MOORE, freelance writer and consultant

"*Prove It* is something amazing: a brief but comprehensive instruction manual for truth in marketing. If you hate bullshit, you'd better read this ... and put it into practice."
JOSH BERNOFF, bestselling author, *Writing Without Bullshit*

"Modern marketing has been elevated to a new level... know, like, trust, and *proof*. The title of this book says it all—and the content of this book teaches it all. A classic."

MIKE MICHALOWICZ, author, *Get Different* and *Profit First*

"If you want higher quality leads that are easier to convert, your marketing and messaging must be excellent. In *Prove It*, Melanie Deziel and Phil M Jones provide an easy-to-follow framework that increases the quality of your leads by positioning your company as the most transparent and trustworthy option."

CHRIS SMITH, author, *The Conversion Code*

"If you want to rise above the noise, give your customers something they don't hear often—*proof*! More referrals, more testimonials, and more customer loyalty are waiting for you. A quick read with a big impact."

TODD HERMAN, author, *The Alter Ego Effect*; creator, 90 Day Year

"This book provides a mighty one-two punch with Melanie Deziel introducing important concepts for today's business environment and Phil M Jones offering actionable strategies we can implement right away! *Prove It* is an essential read to understand today's well-informed—and rightfully skeptical—consumers and stakeholders."

JEFFREY SHAW, author, *The Self-Employed Life*

"Finally, a book without the content fluff. The specifics in *Prove It* will help anyone with any means become a leading expert in their field."

JOE PULIZZI, founder, The Tilt and CEX

"It wasn't too long ago that prospects automatically trusted you unless given a reason not to. But today, they visit your website or walk into any potential transaction with their guard firmly up. *Prove It* shares a simple solution to many of today's marketing and sales challenges. It may just be the most practical and timeless marketing book ever written."

OLI LUKE, co-founder, Orange & Gray
and The Business of Hearing

"*Prove It* could have been called *Do This Now to Instantly Improve Your Sales*. The frameworks outlined in this book transcend the social media fads of the day and provide marketers with the essential skills to create sales campaigns that work. The best part *Prove It*? It's easy to implement. After reading this book, you can immediately apply the lessons you've learned to drive better results for your business. This is the marketing book you don't want your competition to read."

JIMMY MACKIN, CEO, Curaytor

"Finally, a book that demonstrates that successful marketing is all about earning *trust*!"

DAVID HORSAGER, CEO, Trust Edge Leadership Institute

"Businesses that differentiate on trust and truth create competitive advantage. This book is, quite literally, the proof of how brands become a trusted source of interesting things, and what separates those brands from the pack."

ROBERT ROSE, founder, The Content Advisory

PROVE IT

PROVE IT

IT
Exactly How
Modern Marketers
Earn Trust

MELANIE DEZIEL
WITH PHIL M JONES

●● PAGE TWO

Cataloguing in publication information is
available from Library and Archives Canada.
ISBN 978-1-77458-201-5 (paperback)
ISBN 978-1-77458-202-2 (ebook)

Page Two
pagetwo.com

Edited by Melissa Edwards
Copyedited by Jenny Govier
Proofread by Alison Strobel
Cover, interior design, and illustrations by Fiona Lee
Printed and bound in Canada by Friesens
Distributed in Canada by Raincoast Books
Distributed in the US and internationally by Macmillan

22 23 24 25 26   5 4 3 2 1

peoplewhoproveit.com

This book is dedicated to your customers,
who will soon know just how dedicated you are to them.

Contents

Introduction by Phil M Jones *1*

PART I **WHERE'S THE PROOF?**

1 **The Case for Evidence** *5*

2 **How Trust Works** *13*

3 **The Five Claim Types** *19*

4 **Building a Body of Evidence** *29*

PART II **HOW TO PROVE IT**

5 **Proving Convenience** *45*

6 **Proving Comparability** *61*

7 **Proving Commitment** *75*

8 **Proving Connection** *91*

9 **Proving Competence** *107*

Conclusion:
Are You Ready to Prove It? *119*

Acknowledgments *123*

Notes *125*

Introduction

BY PHIL M JONES

THE VERY first time I was introduced to Melanie Deziel, it was in fact before I had even met her. Her headshot and the topic, title, and description of her speech at a large upcoming conference just leaped off the screen. In a sea of speakers claiming a commitment to providing the new secret to ABC or the winning formula to XYZ, Melanie was inviting us to "Think Like a Journalist."

This curiosity-sparking title captured my imagination and instantly began to reframe my thinking on how businesses, leaders, and practitioners really choose to communicate. She was right: gone are the days of making bold, audacious claims and expecting consumers to buy them. All of us now live in a world full of noise, full of promises—and the only way to stand out from that clutter is to focus your effort and energy on collecting and presenting assets that deliver the proof that we are what we say we are.

Months after that moment, Melanie and I met in real life and began a never-ending discussion on what it really takes to win today. That discussion has led to an evolution in how I approach my own business-building activities and the strategies I implement for my clients. It has changed the way I think about marketing *forever*.

The problem for most marketers today is not a lack of ideas or opportunities, but instead a lack of resources and focus. The latest shiny object can easily distract, and with the plethora of new platforms and the rise of FOMO (fear of missing out) connected to the relentless demands of being on trend with the latest and greatest, it can be all too easy to find yourself insanely chasing your tail but not really accomplishing anything that truly moves the needle.

One thing I feel certain of, and why this book matters today more than ever, is that the need for businesses to create content that attracts, converts, retains, and educates their audiences will be here for the foreseeable future. Amid the throngs of largely pointless "look at me" assets being created and the experts telling you to simply re-purpose your content everywhere you can, this book is providing an alternative, smarter approach: to *pre-purpose* your efforts, so that you can achieve a lot more return with a lot less effort.

PHIL M JONES

PART I

WHERE'S THE PROOF?

The Case
for Evidence

So MUCH of the sales process—including all of the marketing that supports it—is focused on reassuring prospects that we are what we say we are, and that we do what we say we do. That imperative can lead to some pretty bold claims:

- "We'll get you the fastest results, guaranteed."

- "No other widget on the market is easier to use."

- "We will do whatever it takes to help you succeed."

- "All of our ingredients are locally sourced, GMO-free, and organic."

- "We've got more than 100 years of experience."

With each of these declarations, we're claiming that we're the best in the business. That we're the best to work with. That we care, and that we're better than any alternative they may be considering.

In most cases, though, all we're really saying to consumers is this: "Just trust us."

But here's the thing. They don't.

Consumers are finding it difficult to trust companies, as more than three-quarters of respondents from the US (77%), the UK (79%), and Spain (79%) report this growing mistrust. Distrust is particularly problematic in France, Canada, Australia, Italy, and India, where more than 8 in 10 respondents are increasingly skeptical. That compares with China, somewhat of an outlier in there being only 55% of respondents finding it more difficult to trust what a company says or the actions it takes. (MarketingCharts)

And who can blame them? In a world full of fraud, scams, and shady businesses—just take a look at your own spam folder or missed call list to see a small sampling—why should any prospective customer trust us before they've tried us? The advertising, marketing, and sales industry isn't exactly thought of as honest, trustworthy, and objective. In fact, sort of the opposite:

Advertising is associated with selling and often leans toward exaggerating... As claims are becoming more complicated and more difficult to substantiate, consumers today are more likely to be skeptical toward advertising. (Carl Obermiller et al., *Journal of Advertising*)

While *we* might not be out to deceive our customers and prospects, there are plenty of people who are. The European Commission estimates that "a total of approximately

24 billion EUR of financial losses resulting from scams and fraud [were] incurred by the EU adult population over a two-year period." Australian consumers lost more than $8 million to online shopping scams, more than $17 million to false billing, and more than $177 million to investment scams in 2021. In the United States alone, consumers lost more than $3.3 billion to fraud in 2020, with $246 million of that coming from online shopping scams specifically.

By maintaining a healthy bit of skepticism with all their potential purchases and service engagements, consumers are simply making a logical choice to protect themselves.

Where Sales, Marketing, and Customer Experience Meet

When faced with a skeptical audience, the last thing you want to do is dictate to them what they should think or feel. Before working with businesses, I was a journalist, and one of the first things that journalists learn is "show, don't tell." Instead of saying "This is bad" or "This is good," a skilled journalist aims to collect all of the data points relevant to a story, distill them down to the most important pieces, and use those facts to paint a picture so detailed that the audience can draw an informed conclusion on their own.

I've spent my entire career working to bring this "show, don't tell" mentality into the world of business communications. I served as the first-ever editor of branded content at *The New York Times*, where I coached our advertisers on how to create compelling content that our audience would value. As a consultant, I've helped Fortune 100 companies implement content strategies that focus more on the audience's needs and interests than on their lifetime value as a customer. And I've been lucky enough to stand on stages around the world, delivering keynotes and workshops on this very topic to audiences filled with sales professionals, small business owners, and marketers from every industry, background, and walk of life.

It was through the community of professional speakers that I first met Phil M Jones, whom you heard from in the introduction to this book and whose contributions and ideas you will find in each chapter to come. We initially bonded over a shared love of our craft, but the more we chatted about our work, our families, and our lives, the more we became less like speaker friends and more like friends.

Phil and his wife, Charlotte, attended my wedding in 2018, and Charlotte quickly became one of my closest friends too. Phil provided invaluable advice and support as I grew my business and wrote my first book, and I got to cheer him on from the front row as he made his Broadway debut. In 2019, my husband and I visited Phil and Charlotte at the hospital after the birth of their beautiful twin girls, and we came to visit regularly in the weeks that followed. Yasin and I welcomed a daughter of our own a few months later. We were lucky to see our three little ones crawl and play together before the world shut down in 2020, and they had more than a few FaceTime and Zoom playdates through the months that followed.

Even when it wasn't our goal, our conversation would often find its way back to our professional lives. I was working with marketers and Phil was working with sales professionals, but we were both determined to shift attention back to the customers and to convince others to prioritize the needs and challenges of consumers. We came to realize that the same strategy that can win your customers' attention through marketing can also win their confidence in a sales context: all you have to do is give them the proof that they're looking for.

If you want consumers to lower their guard enough to trust you—and hence to do business with you—then you need to provide enough *evidence* to set your claims apart from the sea of marketing and sales messages they're attempting to wade through. You might think that "evidence" seems like an overly formal word to use in a discussion about acquiring new customers. I mean, for those of us who work in sales, marketing, and customer experience, we like to think of what we do as *relationship building*, not lawyering. But think about the literal definition of "evidence" as applied in a court of law: it's every type of proof you use in a trial to convince the judge and jury of the facts.

We might not be in a court of law, but we are trying to convince an equally skeptical audience. If we want to prove to those prospects and customers that the claims we make about our products, services, and operations are true, then evidence is exactly what we need to provide. And we can't wait to gather this proof until someone asks for it. Your potential customers are scrolling through your competitors' offerings at breakneck speed. By the time you've prepared your case, they've already made their purchase somewhere else. That means you need to provide evidence to back up your business claims both proactively and frequently.

New Consumers tend to be much less trusting than Old ones. Since they are more suspicious of authority

in general, simply being told that something is the case
fails to impress them. They want to be given concrete
evidence that things are as they are claimed to be before
judging them either credible or unreliable. (David Lewis
and Darren Bridger, *The Soul of the New Consumer*)

In case earning the trust of your customers isn't a compelling enough reason to provide evidence for your business
claims, there's also the law to consider. In the United States,
the Federal Trade Commission Act prohibits "unfair or
deceptive advertising in any medium." By law, a claim
doesn't have to outright lie to be considered misleading—
all it needs to do is leave out relevant information, or even
imply a benefit or quality that it doesn't actually provide. If
you say it, you have to be able to prove it:

Claims must be substantiated, especially when they
concern health, safety, or performance. The type of
evidence may depend on the product, the claims, and
what experts believe necessary. If your ad specifies a
certain level of support for a claim—*"tests show X"*—you
must have at least that level of support. (Federal Trade
Commission)

It's not just in the United States, either. In 2006, the
European Commission issued a directive that stated, "It is
appropriate to enable courts and administrative authorities
to require traders to produce evidence as to the accuracy of
factual claims they have made."

Just as a court can be convinced by evidence, so too
can the minds of skeptical consumers. A claim presented

without evidence falls flat. But a claim presented with sufficient relevant evidence will do exactly what you want it to: give you the edge you need to win trust, convert prospects, and retain customers.

In this book I'm going to discuss the five different types of claims your business is likely making and show you how to provide evidence that proves these claims to be true. Because this process is as much about sales as it is about marketing, Phil will punctuate each chapter with some specific actions, sharing "exactly what to do now" to leverage these insights in a tactical way.

By the end of this book, you'll have the self-awareness you need to create content that proves the truth of each business claim you make. If you can do that, you'll make it impossible for your audience to believe anything else.

Exactly What to Do Now

BY PHIL M JONES

Melanie's insights throughout this book are crafted to be less of a playbook for what to *do* differently than a guide to how to *think* differently about your content creation.

My role is to help you channel that thinking into purposeful actions that will also guide you into operating with a "Prove It" mentality. A word of warning, though: This is a job that is never complete. As market conditions continue to change, you will need to keep evolving your message to meet those conditions. The market is always the biggest influence on your success. That means your job is to feed the market in the most effective way.

The challenge you face in building your own action plan as you read this book is twofold. You are likely to be both inspired by the quantity of ideas you generate *and* paralyzed by the quality required of you if you want to truly achieve the outcome. Move at the pace of the book and treat me as a trusted mentor guiding your actions as we go. At this point, my question for you is narrow and bold: What are the top three truths about you and your organization that, if more people understood them, would have the greatest positive impact?

Perhaps it's your considerable expertise, or the valuable additional service you provide. Or perhaps it's your aftercare, your value for money, your unrivaled quality, your creativity, your proven track record, or something completely different. It's likely there are many such things, but for now narrow it to your *big* three. This focus will help you a great deal. There will always be future opportunities to revisit any other claims you are looking to prove.

2

How Trust Works

EVEN WHEN marketers, sales professionals, and business owners have the absolute best of intentions, most of us still don't do a very good job of backing up our business claims. Often, when asked to expand on a claim or provide more context, we simply repeat the claim, or at best rephrase it.

But that's not how you win consumer trust.

Consumer trust refers to "the expectations held by the consumer that the service provider is dependable and can be relied upon to deliver on its promises." In other words, consumer trust is the degree to which consumers believe that you are what you say you are and that you'll do what you say you'll do. Naturally, having trust in an organization (or an individual representing it) would positively affect a consumer's likelihood of doing business with them. We don't typically rush to do business with people or organizations we *don't* trust.

When a consumer trusts an organization enough to do business with them and then has an experience that matches their expectations, that trust begins to evolve into loyalty. When expectations are met, it's reasonable to assume they'll be met again. So if a consumer's trust hasn't been broken, there's little reason to take a gamble on a different provider who hasn't proven themselves trustworthy yet. But before a prospect can become a loyal customer, we need to first prove ourselves to be trustworthy enough for that initial transaction.

In many industries, consumers don't have to rely on trust alone when choosing a service provider. If they go into a restaurant, they can feel confident that it's clean because the local health authorities have licensed it. If they step into an elevator, they can feel safe knowing they'll be lifted up 78 floors by a device that has been built to code and certified. When they go to a beautician, they know that the law says those clippers must be sterilized and those brushes must be cleaned. In these industries and many others, official governing bodies perform inspections or administer tests to verify these things, the results of which are posted prominently as evidence for anyone who cares to look.

As business owners, it's our job to ensure that proof of our claims can be just as easily discovered, even if it's not required by law. Because if we want our audience to believe the things we say—to trust us, to choose us—then we need to show our audience that our claims are true.

Proving It, with Purpose

In my book *The Content Fuel Framework: How to Generate Unlimited Story Ideas*, I break down the 10 most common content focuses and story formats that can be used to bring

your marketing ideas to life. But this type of content marketing is not just a way to find and connect with our potential
customers. It's also one of the most natural and effective
ways for businesses to validate our claims, and to show—not
tell—those customers that what we say about our business
claims is true.

Admittedly, "content marketing" has become a bit of
a buzzword in recent years—it's an approach to marketing
that, as the Content Marketing Institute says, "is focused on
creating and distributing valuable, relevant, and consistent
content to attract and retain a clearly defined audience—
and, ultimately, to drive profitable customer action." But
in today's multi-platform world, defining "content" is not
always easy. Take the 10 formats I lay out in *The Content Fuel
Framework*: writing, infographics, audio, video, live-stream
video, image galleries, timelines, quizzes, tools, and maps.
Each one of these formats contains multitudes: audio can be
everything from a podcast to a recording of ambient sound,
and a tool can be anything from a calculator to a name gen-
erator. (Don't even get me started on all the ways you can
use "writing.") But these are just the beginning. The term
"content" encompasses any idea shared through any print or
digital medium for audience consumption, and that means
it can include everything from a text message, Instagram
post, or FAQ page to an online course, comic strip, or entire
feature-length film like *The LEGO Movie*. And each one of
these formats can be leveraged to make your case—to present your evidence to your audience. The key is to focus on
substance.

See, the conversation in too many conference rooms
focuses on "what to post," and not on "what to post *about*."
Content has so much power, but many businesses simply

use it as fluff. It's become a commodity, measured by frequency rather than effectiveness, and celebrated for form rather than function. But when we decide on the content delivery method before we figure out what we're actually delivering, we end up with a poor match between the story and the format. We end up with a 15-page white paper that should have been a 300-word blog post—and, at worst, one that leaves the reader struggling to understand what the point of it was. It's not unlike choosing a gigantic shipping box before you know what needs to go inside it: you end up · with a lot of filler, a lot of wasted space and resources, and a recipient who wonders if the person who put it all together actually knows what they're doing.

There's nothing magical about a "publish," "post," or "upload" button that can automatically translate into leads, customers, or sales. For the content to make a meaningful difference in your business—for it to be the evidence your customers need to believe the claims you make—it needs to have both purpose and substance. It must be clearly aligned with broader business goals, and it needs to say something worth hearing.

Or, as Ben Franklin put it in his 1738 *Poor Richard's Almanack*:

> If you would not be forgotten
> As soon as you are dead and rotten
> Either write things worth reading
> Or do things worth the writing.

The best content marketing *shows* the audience that our businesses and our offerings are worthy of their time, money, and attention. The best content acts as proof for a business claim and helps our prospects and customers gain trust that we are every bit as valuable as we say we are. When we provide evidence of our business claims, we help eliminate consumer doubt, which removes one of the largest obstacles we're up against as marketers and business owners.

We are the defendants in this case. The burden of proof is on us. Let's prepare our case.

Exactly What to Do Now

BY PHIL M JONES

One factor that influences trust more than almost anything else is consistency. How you show up consistently is how you become trusted to show up. No doubt you know one person who is always late to meetings. Eventually, you trust them to always be late.

Before you begin rapidly building your case to increase trust with consumers, be certain that what you are choosing to do is something you feel committed to doing for the long term, and not just for a sprint. The restaurant with hundreds of five-star reviews gathered in a three-month window but no new reviews posted since 2019 is only proving that it *used* to be great, not that it *is* great.

This book will soon have you energized to collect and generate evidence everywhere. So to prevent yourself from getting too creative in too many directions, it makes sense to first draw some of your own boundaries and decide where your own content strengths lie. Knowing where to focus your attention will give you confidence that you can truly create with consistency in your chosen medium.

The Five
Claim Types

USINESSES MAKE an endless array of claims: we vouch for our product, our people, our process, our service, and more. And we make these claims in an equally endless array of ways and places.

When I talk about a "business claim," I'm referring to any communication that promises, guarantees, or sets an expectation in the minds of your prospects, customers, or anyone else with whom your company interacts. If your organization has a clearly identified brand promise, that promise will—by definition—include some sort of claim about what consumers can expect from the way you operate. Two of the most common forms these promises take are the *tagline* and the *slogan*.

Some taglines and catchphrases include a guarantee, as with Geico's "15 minutes could save you 15% or more on car insurance." But since taglines and slogans are often created to attract or entertain consumers more than to convert them, many don't include an actual business claim. Wendy's "Where's the beef?" catchphrase, for example, doesn't make any real promises that need proof.

A company's list of values will commonly include multiple brand promises. American Express, for example, includes "We do what's right" as one of their core values, saying, "Customers choose us because they trust our brand and people. We earn that trust by ensuring everything we do is reliable, consistent, and with the highest level of integrity." While company values like these are primarily intended to govern internal behavior and policies, these statements also set an expectation for the consumer.

But there's a good chance that most of the claims you and your business are making are happening in a much less formal capacity. These claims might be found in your advertisements, hidden in your website copy, spoken aloud by your associates, printed on your packaging, or even presented on a sign that's likely hanging in your restroom right now. (Is there a business out there that *doesn't* take pride in the cleanliness of its restrooms?) And, while it may be less public than some of the splashier claim types, your fine print is almost certainly packed with claims: warranties, return policies, privacy policies, contracts, terms and conditions, and more.

What Promises Are You Making?

While the specifics of your claims will always be unique to your industry, business, product, and customers, most will fall into one of five categories.

Convenience

Claiming to be convenient means sharing how easy it is to work with you. Convenience claims might include things like ease, proximity, and speed.

If you can prove your product or service is convenient, that's a claim you should make. Consumer research has shown that convenience is now a top priority for more than three-quarters of consumers when they choose a retailer. Show them how you can minimize friction at every point in their customer experience, and you'll go a long way toward convincing them that you're the one to be working with and buying from.

Comparability

Claiming to be comparable means declaring that you measure up well to the competition. These claims might reference things like quality, durability, and effectiveness.

Proving comparability is key in a world where consumers have access to more options than ever. According to a study on comparison shopping, 95% of online shoppers visit at least two websites before finalizing a purchase, and 51% check out four or more sites. Online, there is no way to pretend that you're the only option, so you should instead focus on providing evidence that you deserve to be at the top of their list.

Commitment

Claiming to be committed means providing reassurance that you are worthy of trust and that you operate ethically. This type of claim frequently references things like transparency, fairness, procedural goals, and a promise to protect people, private data, property, or the environment.

Proving your commitment—both to others and to your own values—is no longer optional. Almost three-quarters of consumers say they prefer buying from companies that share their values, and the younger the consumer, the more this is true: 83% of millennials prefer to buy from brands that are aligned with their values, and 76% of 18- to 34-year-olds like it when leaders from the companies they buy from speak out on issues they care about. If you can prove your commitment to the values you claim to have and the issues your customers care about, you can earn the favor of conscious shoppers who want to do business with companies they can get behind.

Connection

Claiming to be connected means proclaiming that you prioritize close relationships. These claims relate to your loyalty, your role in the community, and the level of care you provide for your customers.

Despite the fact that many purchases happen online with relatively little human interaction, 56% of consumers say they are more likely to shop at a retailer that recognizes them by name, whether that's in a brick-and-mortar shop or online. Companies that can prove they are connected are differentiating themselves in a world of anonymous superstores and corporate service providers that see each customer as just a set of numbers in a database.

Competence

Claiming to be competent means stating that you are capable of delivering on what's promised. These claims typically relate to qualifications, reliability, and consistency.

It almost goes without saying that you should be delivering quality on a consistent basis, but sadly that's not always the case. It's no surprise, then, that 73% of global consumers say they trust a brand based on its ability to deliver good-quality products or services. Proving that you are capable of delivering at the level you've promised is fundamental to earning consumer trust, business, and loyalty.

IN PART II, we'll explore each of these five business claims in more depth and show you what evidence you need to provide to prove each type to your customers. But first, let's run through a few strategies you can use to find out exactly what claims you are making—because you might be saying more than you think.

Identifying Your Claims

Before we can prove it, we need to know what "it" is. So, to make sure you get the most out of this book, let's take some time to identify exactly what claims your business is making and where you are making them.

The first step is to review the information in every possible place where your business might be communicating to your prospects and customers. Here's where you should start:

Your website: Spend a lot of time here, because this is the central repository for information about your business. Don't stop at the home page: examine your "company history," "customer service," and "about" pages; your pop-up messages; and your blog posts. Pay particular attention to your product pages and pages promoting specific offers.

Your advertisements: Your company's ads—whether physical or digital—almost always include business claims. Look at the wording and imagery being used for any digital display advertising, newspaper ads, flyers, billboards, television ads, radio ads, and direct mailers, as well as any other ads or sponsorships.

Your printed material: This is another common place for business claims, so review your product packaging, business cards, brochures, pamphlets, catalogs, letterhead, and more. Don't forget your business materials, such as contracts, invoices, and receipts, and any trade show materials, like banners, counter cards, and table toppers.

Your digital communications: Look for any claims you make in your sales or presentation slides, onboarding videos and communications, email newsletters, and social media, as well as any transaction confirmations you provide.

Your physical location: If you have a physical location, you'll want to have a thorough look around to see if there are any additional claims being made in places your customers can access. Consider storefronts, waiting areas, offices, showrooms, conference rooms, kiosks, and other experiential spaces. Examine your in-store displays, all of your signage, any slogans on the walls, your price labels, and even the uniforms on your staff.

Your reviews and ratings: As hard as it may be, you should also make a point of seeking out any instances of negative feedback from reviews, ratings, surveys, and comment cards. While some of the experiences you see described are not actually claims being made by you, they can be a very good measure of whether you are accidentally making claims you may not even be aware of. Often, a negative experience is the result of mismanaged expectations: the customer expected one thing and got something else entirely.

In all these forms of business communication, certain words can act like signposts or clues that you've stumbled upon a claim. The most obvious words to look for as you review your information are those five claim types we've covered: convenience, comparability, commitment, connection, and competence. Don't forget to look for synonyms: words like "experienced," "certified," and "knowledgeable" can stand in for "competent," and "easy," "quick," and "instant" can stand in for "convenient."

Many claims include obvious signal words like "promise" and "guarantee." And any time you see something followed by the phrase "or your money back," you can be sure you're looking at a business claim. Other words associated with claims include "assure," "expect," "pledge," "vow," and "oath." Absolute language is often used to set expectations, so scan for words like "never," "always," "none," "all," "only," and related terms. Similarly, look for language that refers to limitations, such as "exclude," "include," "except," "maximum," and "minimum."

Looking for numbers will also help you identify a claim. Examples are qualifiers like "in 30 minutes or less," "after 14 days," and "for at least five years." You'll also want to keep an eye out for superlatives: "best," "most," "fastest," "easiest," and "oldest," for example. In fact, almost any adjective—quick, clean, fresh, hot, friendly, durable—means that an expectation is being presented to your audience.

Once you've completed this business claim "audit" and compiled your list of claims, it's time to categorize them according to the five claim types. Then, in Part II, I'll show you how to take a strategic approach to identifying the evidence that will best prove the validity for claims in each category.

How Provable Are Your Claims?

As you think critically about all the claims that your business is making, it's also helpful to categorize those claims as objective or subjective.

Objective claims can be easily proven or disproven by standard measurement systems. It is easy for your customer (or a certifying body) to determine the truth about whether your product really has three attachments, or comes in 14 colors, or has only three grams of sugar, or lasts for six weeks. Many objective claims are quantitative—that is, they include a number that can be counted—but some claims can also be assessed in non-numerical ways. Does a product really fold flat? Is it really waterproof? Does it really leave no residue behind? These types of objective "yes/no" claims can be measured or tested for a clear and repeatable outcome: fold it, drop it in water, use it and check for residue.

Subjective claims, by contrast, are more difficult to prove: perhaps the way they are measured is not standardized, or there's no way to measure the characteristic in question, or the definitions of the words used in the claim can differ depending on who is reading them. There aren't exactly common scales to measure how modern, bold, stylish, helpful, adorable, or tasty something is. (Is "yummy" better than "tasty"? Where does "delicious" fit in? How do all those rank against "scrumptious"?) A certain fabric might be soft to one consumer but scratchy to another. Products that I find beautiful or useful, you may find tacky or pointless.

Studies have shown that consumers are somewhat less skeptical about objective claims, likely because they believe that the measurability means that someone, somewhere would have called the product out if the claims were false. Since subjective claims are harder to measure, they tend to create a bit more skepticism—and that means you may need content that brings in multiple and even outside opinions.

Keep these distinctions between objective claims and subjective claims in mind as you move through the chapters that follow. Ultimately, regardless of whether your claims are objective or subjective, providing the appropriate proof will allow you to increase a customer's degree of certainty about the truth of your claims, which ultimately increases the likelihood that they'll be willing to take the leap and do business with you.

One final word of warning: As you move through this process and reflect on how to build a body of evidence for each claim on your list, you may discover that some of your claims are not actually as true as you thought. Should this happen— should you discover that one of your claims doesn't have the evidence you need to back it up—don't panic. That's OK.

It's more than OK, actually. Consider it a blessing—an unexpected benefit of going through this process of identifying your claims and creating the evidence you need to prove their truth. After all, it's far better for *you* to discover that some of your current claims lack evidence than for your prospects or customers to discover it first. (Mind you, if your claims aren't true and you know it, I recommend exploring the "ethics" or "self-improvement" sections at your favorite bookseller.)

If you do find gaps between your claims and their provability, you have two options. Most obviously, you can take steps to adapt your practices and products to ensure that you live up to those claims in the future. But you can also adjust your claims to reflect the more reliable and provable truth.

That's what proving it is all about: providing the evidence to ensure that your audience comes to an accurate verdict about the ways in which you can provide value to them.

Exactly What to Do Now

BY PHIL M JONES

Completing a claims audit is not the simplest thing to do. To make life easier—and to learn how much more purposeful you can be with your claims—try benchmarking the claims you are already making for your business with the resources Melanie and I have provided for you on our website: peoplewhoproveit.com.

What you may soon realize is that it is not only possible to amplify your existing claims so that they have more impact, but it is also likely you should be making *further* claims in other key areas.

4

Building a
Body of Evidence

Now that we know that content is a great means of providing evidence for the claims we make about our products and services, it's time to examine how exactly that process works.

There are three ways you can use content as evidence: through corroboration, through demonstration, and through education. Let's take a closer look at each.

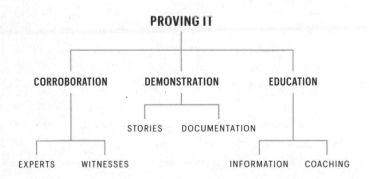

PROVING IT

CORROBORATION   DEMONSTRATION   EDUCATION

STORIES   DOCUMENTATION

EXPERTS   WITNESSES   INFORMATION   COACHING

Proving by Corroborating

When you corroborate your business claims, you use other people's perspectives to validate your own. In the marketing world, we call this third-party credibility or social proof.

There are two primary options for who could provide that corroboration: experts and witnesses. Both lend credibility to your claims, but they do so in different ways.

Experts

Your expert corroborators bring an informed perspective. Experts might be academics, researchers, long-time practitioners, inspectors, authors, or other influencers who have a higher-than-average level of knowledge of the space.

At the most basic level, using experts as proof of your claims involves including their quotes, assessments, recommendations, and findings in your content. Whether you decide to share these expert insights on your website, product packaging, in-store signage, social media feeds, or somewhere else, you're making it easy for consumers to find an assessment by someone knowledgeable to help with their decision-making process.

While "experts" may sound inherently human, you can also corroborate your claims with non-human evidence that has been conveyed by human experts, such as rankings, awards, or certifications. The *Fortune* list of the "World's Most Admired Companies," for example, is compiled after asking "executives, directors, and analysts to rate enterprises in their own industry on nine criteria, from investment value and quality of management and products to social responsibility and ability to attract talent." The aggregate ratings of qualified experts give consumers an overall picture of what those experts think of the companies and how they stack up against their competitors.

These types of industry awards and rankings are certainly good for your ego, and they have been proven to benefit recruitment, employee morale, brand awareness, and brand credibility. But the impact of this type of third-party proof extends to your bottom line too. A study by operations management professors from Georgia Institute of Technology and the College of William and Mary showed that award-winning companies "significantly outperformed" non-winning companies on a number of key metrics. Over a five-year period, companies that earned awards for quality experienced

* a 42% greater increase in total assets,

* a 37% higher jump in sales,

* 16% more employee growth,

* an 8% higher return on sales, and

* a 3% higher return on assets.

The same study showed that publicly traded award winners beat the S&P 500 index by a full 34%.

It's important to note that "expert" is a relative term, ultimately defined more by your prospects and customers than by you. Who a consumer trusts to give expert recommendations can depend on the type of product or service, the price point, and the relative stakes of the decision. I don't know about you, but I'd be much more likely to seek out highly credentialed experts when deciding whether or not to have an expensive and potentially dangerous medical procedure than I would when deciding between two brands of sandwich bread.

In most contexts that require specialized education or credentials—medicine, science, technology, economics, and more—the definition of "expert" generally involves academic professionals and researchers. A global study by PR firm Edelman showed that 59% of consumers rate academic experts as very credible or extremely credible sources of information about a company. But when it comes to more personalized and experiential contexts—like food, fashion, or beauty—the experts look a little bit different. For example, a Harvard Business School study found that social media influencers are some of the most trusted experts in the beauty industry. Whether these online personalities were creating makeup tutorial videos for YouTube or listing recommended products in the captions of perfectly styled Instagram photos, nearly 67% of women surveyed trusted these influencers' opinions more than any other source.

And who comes next in the list of trusted sources for beauty recommendations? Your peers. In fact, 59% of the women surveyed trusted third-party reviews from consumers just like them.

Witnesses

This type of corroborator can include customers, clients, vendors, members, attendees, employees, students, buyers, or whoever else may have personally tested the truth of your claim. Witnesses like these are trusted because they share their first-hand experiences, opinions, and recommendations.

Proof provided by witnesses most often comes in the form of testimonials or reviews. In a 2019 *Edelman Trust Barometer* survey, 57% of global respondents and 63% of American respondents said they trust a brand when it gets good ratings and reviews. And a consumer survey from BrightLocal found that 87% of US consumers read online reviews for local businesses—a figure that went up 6 points after the start of the pandemic in 2020. In fact, the survey also showed that the average customer spends about 13 minutes reading reviews before making a decision.

This type of evidence is especially important for more skeptical consumers, who studies have shown rely more heavily on discussions with friends and other peers to validate the claims businesses make. You don't need to provide a ton of this type of content to make a difference in your prospects' buying decisions. A study from Northwestern University found that the purchase likelihood for a product with five reviews is 270% larger than that of a product with zero reviews. So don't be discouraged if you're still in the process of gathering quality reviews—each one helps.

Not only do user reviews inspire consumer trust, but they also affect keyword rankings on search engines. A business with 10 or more reviews can see a 15% to 20% increase in search traffic, which means more customers can find them.

Just as a single review from an individual consumer can serve as witness corroboration, so can the aggregate star rating or survey ranking generated by a collection of reviews. A Harvard Business School study showed that increasing a restaurant's Yelp rating by just one star generates a revenue increase of between 5% and 9%.

Then there's J.D. Power & Associates, which touts itself as the "Voice of the Consumer." The company conducts satisfaction surveys with customers of particular brands and products, creating an aggregate ranking to compare against industry benchmarks and giving out awards that "help companies increase consumer consideration and ensure that highest performing brands stand out in the crowd." J.D. Power has strict guidelines for advertising claims, to make sure their conclusions can't be misrepresented or manipulated by brands with malice. As the company states on its website, "Every advertising claim related to a study is reviewed prior to publication to ensure accuracy."

Proving by Demonstrating

When you demonstrate your business claims, you are providing evidence that your audience can experience for themselves. (Normally I'd say "see" for themselves, but I want to allow for the option of providing this content in audio form, which can be equally compelling.) You can demonstrate the validity of your claims through stories and through documentation.

Stories
Stories provide narrative evidence by walking through a past example. They are probably one of the most common ways that businesses provide proof, and they can include things like case studies, customer profiles, and success stories.

"Now wait a minute," you're probably thinking. "Isn't a case study or a customer success story the same as the reviews and testimonials we just talked about as a form of corroborating evidence?"

Not exactly. Reviews and testimonials typically come directly from the customer—they might be submitted to your website, posted on a third-party platform (think Yelp, Tripadvisor, and G2), shared on a forum, or even passed on through word of mouth. They're often brief, ranging from just a few words to perhaps a few paragraphs if the reviewer is particularly passionate.

By contrast, case studies, customer profiles, and success stories are presented by you, the brand. They are also typically longer, more in-depth, and more narrative driven—meaning they read like a real story. Where a review might simply say: "Worked great. —Sam F.," a case study would use hundreds of words or eight minutes of video to present a detailed story of what Sam was looking for, what else they had tried, how they discovered the brand, what the experience of working with the company was like, and what results they were able to achieve together.

All of this added detail serves to paint a more complete picture of both the customer and the product or service they purchased. This added context can help other consumers see that someone who might have their same challenges, needs, budget, or situation found this solution to be the right one. In one survey by Wyzowl, two-thirds of consumers reported being more likely to make a purchase after watching a testimonial video demonstrating how a business, product, or service helped someone similar to them.

Documentation

Providing documentation allows the audience—the jury—to see the proof with their own eyes and hear it with their own ears. "Seeing is believing," as they say, and content that demonstrates the truth of your business claims allows your audience to observe the validity of those claims on their own.

Documentation often comes in the form of photos and videos that have been captured as the story plays out. Live video streaming can be a very effective form of documentation because of how much more difficult it is to edit than a pre-recorded video; this extra level of reliability helps to further cut through customer skepticism. But your documentation doesn't necessarily need to be broadcast to your audience live.

One common type of documentation is behind-the-scenes content that brings your audience into a place or process they wouldn't otherwise be able to access or experience. In fact, behind-the-scenes content is the second-most-viewed type of content on Instagram, coming in right behind tutorials. Behind-the-scenes content might involve taking the audience into the office, workshop, kitchen, factory, exam room, locker room, stock room, or whatever other location they may not otherwise be able to see. By sharing behind-the-scenes content like this, you not only make your audience feel like an insider, but you also give them an opportunity to see a real, raw, unfiltered view of the company, which can feel more authentic than a more polished advertising message.

Sometimes, proof in the form of documentation can be a bit more literal: records, reports, transcripts, meeting minutes, audits, test results, financial data, and other forms of printed data that serve as tangible evidence of your claims. Ultimately, regardless of the form it takes, documentation works best as proof when it provides enough detail and context that your audience will feel like they are a witness themselves.

Proving by Educating

The eighth edition of Deloitte's annual *Consumer Review* recommended that businesses "develop content to inform and educate consumers and help them move through the decision process," stating that "arming consumers with the right information helps them move independently through the shopping journey, creates trust and increases their loyalty." When brands create content that educates their audience, it increases both trust and brand affinity. Beyond the relational benefits, consumers are also 131% more likely to buy from a brand after consuming educational content.

Most educational content aims to do one of two things: inform or coach.

Informational Content

Informing your audience entails, well... information. Here, you're providing your potential customers with references, product background, definitions, context, or other information that they can use to feel more knowledgeable about the product, the industry, or a specific use case.

Ideally, informational content should help the audience feel like they are more prepared to engage with your brand. Sometimes, informational content is directly tied to your offering, such as content that explains the features of your product or that goes into detail about what your services include. Other times, though, informational content can be more "brand-adjacent." For example, some consumers may need a primer on industry terms and acronyms before they can feel confident in making a purchase or creating a relationship. Maybe they're unsure of what their options are and need a detailed breakdown of the various solutions to their problem that are available on the market. Regardless of what it is that you are teaching your audience, informational content should always be included in your marketing plans: according to KPMG, 41% of consumers say they trust companies that educate them about product features and benefits.

Another type of informational content that works well as a form of proof is thought leadership: first-person or opinion content that comes straight from the leaders of your organization. This kind of content can offer your customers better insight into the way that your leadership team thinks or operates—straight from the horse's mouth. By providing this insight, you are creating an opportunity for a more personal, more human connection with your audience.

Coaching Content

Acting as a coach involves educating your audience about processes that are relevant to your claim. This type of content provides information in the form of guiding, tutoring, or training, providing the steps needed to get a desired outcome.

For example, you might offer a tutorial on how to set up your product, a guide to repairs, or an explainer on how to use your product correctly. Things like recipes, tutorials, and instruction manuals fall into the "coaching" category too. Not all coaching content addresses a physical process, though. You might also create content that coaches your prospects through an important decision, a mindset shift, an emotional transformation, or some other less tangible process.

One of the biggest clues that a piece of content is playing a coaching role is the inclusion of the phrase "how to." If a piece of content describes *how to* make, fix, decide, remove, change, or just about any other verb, then you're almost certainly looking at a piece of coaching content.

Coaching content tends to work well as video, especially in cases where you need a combination of voice and imagery to be able to properly follow along with the process. In fact, research by Google shows that "how to" videos earn the most attention on YouTube, even more than videos about music or gaming.

Combining All Three Types of Evidence

Your instinct may be to choose one of these types of evidence—corroboration, demonstration, or education—and focus on using just that one type to build credibility in the eyes of your consumers. But the truth is that one type of evidence alone likely won't do it.

No single type of content is better or worse than another at proving the validity of your business claims. Each provides value in its own way, and each can be used to support the claims you're making in different ways. Ideally, your business will employ all three types of evidence in *some* way, depending on the context, the audience, and the specific claim you're hoping to prove true.

As we walk through the five different types of provable business claims—convenience, comparability, commitment, connection, and competence—we'll show how each of the three evidential content types we've just discussed can be used to support that specific claim.

Exactly What to Do Now

BY PHIL M JONES

In my world, I often think about my HPAS (high-payoff activities) and then give attention to the actions that are likely to make the biggest impact. At this point, your HPA is to purposefully create a series of lists in six key areas:

LIST 1: Who are the external thought leaders or influencers you could collaborate with to help *amplify* your claims?

LIST 2: Who are the key people that have experienced your products or services that could best *validate* those claims?

LIST 3: What are the specific case studies required to help *display* the historical fulfillment of your claims?

LIST 4: What photos, images, or videos are missing that could help *illustrate* the truth of your claims?

LIST 5: What questions are regularly asked of you that you could easily *answer* with your content?

LIST 6: Where are people meeting difficulties in their efforts to *implement* your products or services?

With these lists in progress, you are building a never-ending treasure map of opportunities to act with more purpose in your content creation and curation.

PART II

HOW TO PROVE IT

5

Proving Convenience

"UNABLE TO modify reservation. Please try again."

I desperately needed to change an upcoming flight to an earlier one, but the airline's website kept giving me this error. After multiple failed attempts, I finally got a pop-up suggesting that I call customer service for assistance.

I dialed the customer service line and was greeted with an automated voice notifying me that my estimated wait time was one hour. There wasn't even an option to request a callback instead of waiting on hold. *Great.*

Slotted in among the rotation of hold music and promotions, there was one message that encouraged me to try texting their customer support chatbot for faster help. I was skeptical that an automated chatbot would be able to give me the help I was looking for, but after 90 minutes on hold, I decided to give it a try. I switched to speakerphone and texted the chatbot.

The bot started the exchange by asking what I needed help with, offering me four options:

A) Changing a flight
B) Canceling a flight
C) Missing a flight
D) Something else

I typed back "A" in reply.

"I'm sorry, I'm still learning and don't fully understand your question."

I hadn't asked a question; I had provided one of the answer options the bot had given me.

So, I tried again. I ended up having to answer that same question three more times. Twice I got a little further along in the "conversation," only to have the bot "not fully understand" another response, sending me back to start all over again.

After 45 minutes of painfully inefficient back-and-forth, the chatbot told me that the easiest way to modify my flight was via the airline's website. Yes, the very same website that had given me an error message in the first place, and then told me to call customer service . . . which, in turn, had told me to use the chatbot.

Luckily, I *had* stayed on hold in the background while texting with the support bot. As my call time crossed the three-hour mark, I started to wonder if the chat was designed merely to keep me occupied while I waited for a representative to answer the call, rather than to provide any real support.

After nearly four hours and three different avenues, I was still on hold and still hadn't been able to change my flight. My stomach started to churn as I watched the number of available seats on my desired flight drop to single digits. I let out a heavy sigh, hung up the phone, and bought a ticket for the earlier flight. Presumably, I could still cancel the old ticket that I wouldn't be able to use, but only if I could find a time when I was able to wait on hold for another few hours.

Now, I know that airlines aren't really known for being the most convenient companies to deal with, but this was a real 1-2-3 strikeout:

1 The self-service option on the website wouldn't let me serve myself.

2 The chatbot wasn't any faster, easier, or more effective.

3 The customer service line massively underestimated the wait time.

After having lost four hours and hundreds of dollars to this process, it's hard to imagine that I would willingly book a flight with this airline again. I've received fast and efficient customer service from many other airlines, so I know *that* level of inconvenience isn't a necessary evil.

Claiming to be *convenient* is making a promise to your customers that their interactions with you will be frictionless. You are telling your audience that the experience of working with you or using your products will be—at the very least—painless, and ideally pleasant. Data from the National Retail Federation shows that 52% of consumers say convenience influences at least half of their purchases, and that greater than 9 out of 10 consumers are more likely to choose a retailer based on convenience. And this trend holds true across industries: the same study showed that 66% of consumers expressed a willingness to pay more for convenience when buying groceries, with the same sentiment being expressed for buying clothing (61% of consumers), electronics (59%), personal care items (58%), and pet supplies (58%).

Types of Convenience Claims

"Convenience" can mean different things to different consumers and in different industries: speed, ease of use, simplicity, availability, accessibility, compatibility, and more. Let's take a look at three of the most common.

Speed claims address the desire for consumers to save time by promising an expedient checkout process, delivery, setup, completion, or outcome. Business claims that emphasize speed often include a specific metric, which makes the claim both easy to understand and easy to measure. Here are a few real-life examples of speed-based claims:

> "15 minutes could save you 15% or more on car insurance."—Geico

> "30 minutes, or it's free."—Domino's Pizza

> "Transform your body from regular to ripped in just 90 days."—P90X

Ease-of-use claims are those that address your consumers' concerns about or frustrations with complexity. These claims could refer to the simplicity of using the product, acquiring the product, completing the purchase, or processing a return.

This type of convenience is especially important for e-commerce businesses—or any business that processes purchases online. Ease of use needs to be a priority at every stage of the purchase process. Data shows that 28% of consumers who abandoned online shopping carts complained about having to create an account, and 21% blamed a complicated or lengthy checkout process. In one study, a whopping 95% of consumers said that convenient delivery options are a major factor in their choice of online retailer. And, knowing that there is a risk that their purchase won't end up being the right fit for them, the customers in that study also wanted this same convenient experience for returns. Nearly 9 in 10 consumers said they don't want to have to deal with the customer service department to make a return, and almost half said they were more likely to shop with brands that offer self-service returns.

Here are some real-life examples of ease-of-use claims:

"Free shipping, free returns. All the time."—Nordstrom

"So easy a caveman could do it."—Geico

"Investing for everyone."—Robinhood

"Great writing, simplified."—Grammarly

"We make commerce easy."—Square

Finally, **compatibility claims** help reassure consumers that your product or service will play well with related items from your offerings, or offerings from others. These claims may emphasize the variety of ways in which your product can be used, the volume of systems with which it can be integrated, or the variety of options, accessories, or add-ons that can be paired with it.

Here are some real-life examples of compatibility claims:

> "Everywhere you want to be."—Visa
>
> "Design anything. Publish anywhere."—Canva
>
> "More integrations than anyone."—Zapier

Proving Convenience with Corroboration

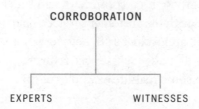

When looking to prove convenience with **expert corroboration**, creating content with influencers can be an incredibly effective approach. Many influencers are seen as authorities in their particular areas of expertise, and their take on your product or service would be seen as trustworthy corroboration of your convenience claims.

Back in 2016, video editing software Adobe Spark partnered with YouTuber Amy Landino for exactly this type of expert corroboration of its benefits. At the time, Amy—who rose to fame under the last name Schmittauer and now shares a name with her husband, fellow influencer Vincenzo Landino—launched a YouTube channel focused on teaching video skills, and she was in the run-up to publishing her first book, *Vlog Like a Boss: How to Kill It Online with Video*

Blogging. With that expertise, an endorsement of a video editing tool like Adobe Spark was perfectly on-brand for Amy and likely to resonate with her audience, many of whom were aspiring vloggers themselves, hoping to replicate her success.

In the nearly nine-minute video, which can be found on YouTube by searching "Beginner Video Editing (That Doesn't Suck)," Amy walks through a tutorial of how her audience can use Adobe Spark for their own video editing, even if they don't have lots of experience. The video includes screen captures of Adobe Spark in action, and a text overlay clearly identifies the video as a paid partnership: "Sponsored: If you're a beginner in video editing, then Adobe Spark just might be the thing you're looking for."

A quick scroll through the comments on the YouTube video shows how well Amy's endorsement of the product's ease of use seems to have worked:

- "Thank you so much. I am a novice at video editing and Adobe Spark looks like it will work for me."

- "Amy, you've been my mentor and teacher throughout my video blog launch—everything I know about vlogging, I learned from you! Thanks for putting out great content as always—will definitely check out Adobe Spark!"

- "The Adobe marketing specialist who asked Amy to partner with them re: their Spark products deserves a raise."

In the years since the video was published, Amy's focus has shifted away from teaching video skills, and she's published hundreds of videos (and even another book) about other topics. And yet, as of 2022, the Adobe Spark video remains her second most popular video ever, with 1.2 million views. People continue to need advice on which video editing tools are easiest for beginners to use, and Amy's video continues to deliver.

Now, I'm not saying you need to go out and find a YouTuber with 400,000+ followers to endorse your product. Instead, I want you to consider the different types of experts who could offer their take on your offering: podcasters, authors, bloggers, social influencers, professors, local celebrities, and so on. Each of these individuals could be a fantastic partner in the creation of content that not only proves the convenience of your product but also potentially creates a lasting relationship that benefits you both.

When it comes to gathering **witness corroboration** on your convenience, though, the most trusted and most accessible witnesses will be your customers. You may already have programs in place to encourage your customers to share their experience with you in surveys after a customer service call or via email, text, or comment cards. In addition to providing you with useful feedback for your business, this type of corroboration can serve as powerful proof of your convenience when it's shared in public forums. This is a good reason to actively encourage your customers to leave reviews mentioning how convenient your product or service is on the third-party ratings sites that are most relevant for your line of business, such as Yelp, Tripadvisor, HomeAdvisor, G2, or DealerRater.

When you have especially positive reviews, find ways to elevate those to help them get seen by more prospects. On many review platforms, replying to a review will help make it more visible, and you may be able to upvote reviews or mark them as "helpful" to help lift them up further. You might also choose to use an image of the review (with the reviewer's permission) in your ads, to feature it prominently on your website, or to amplify that positive response on social media.

Proving Convenience with Demonstration

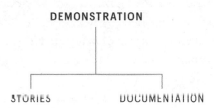

Visa's "everywhere you want to be" tagline helped build its reputation as a ubiquitous and convenient payment option, appealing to consumers who may be concerned about their debit or credit cards being accepted while they're traveling.

But Visa knows that this brand promise is equally important to small business owners, since 97% of shoppers have abandoned a purchase due to a lack of convenience, according to the National Retail Federation. Surely, it's important for small businesses to accept the forms of payment their customers want to use, but being seen as convenient often means embracing additional technology that makes those transactions easier—accepting touchless or mobile payments, for example.

On Visa's company blog, there are countless **stories** showcasing the ways that their payment products and services have helped small businesses around the world. These articles share the stories of the businesses and the passionate teams behind them, helping to paint a more detailed picture of the impact Visa can have on the businesses that use their solution to power some or all of their payments.

A blog post titled "Digital Aid Becomes Lifeline for Unbanked Guatemalans During Pandemic" shares how Visa-powered programs played a role in helping Guatemalan stylist Nancy Gomez reopen her salon. In another—"No Point of Sale? No Problem. Accept Payments with Visa Tap to Phone"—business owners in Peru, Costa Rica, and Malaysia share the impact of being able to accept electronic payments on their phone, without needing a dedicated cash register system.

While Visa's "everywhere you want to be" claim is largely aimed at a cardholding consumer audience, stories like these show that Visa's promise also extends to the small businesses that are everywhere their cardholders want to go.

Convenience can also be proven with content that provides **documentation**. Amy Landino's expert endorsement of Adobe Spark doubles as a demonstration as well as corroboration, since she walked viewers through using the software, showing her screen as she did it. She didn't just *say* that the tool was easy for beginners to use, or tell a story about how easy she found it to be; she actually *showed* how easy it was to use, in real time. You could take a similar approach, walking through how easy your product is to install, set up, clean, repair, or otherwise use.

If you're claiming compatibility, you can create content that documents your product in use with all its possible partner products or systems. This works particularly well for consumer products that can be visually captured. Think of a phone stand photographed holding devices of various types and sizes, or an adjustable wrench shown loosening a variety of nuts and bolts.

If you're claiming speed as your primary convenience, consider using live video as a way to document your efficiency. In a live-stream scenario, you can show the speed of the process as it's happening, with no cuts or edits that might create skepticism in the audience's mind.

Ease-of-use claims can be documented by showing people with varying levels of experience successfully using the product. This is often done at trade shows or in commercials: someone "off the street" is introduced to the product, and viewers can watch as that person uses the product to complete a task or challenge with minimal help.

Proving Convenience with Education

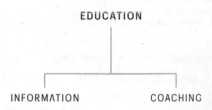

Some types of convenience have obvious value: we all prefer fast delivery to slow delivery, and most of us would opt for simple over complex installation. But educational content can play a particularly important role when your convenience claims are less easily understood.

Take the technology company Zapier, which is billed as "the easiest way to automate your work." This claim isn't a particularly tangible one, though, and it's one that might be

seen as intimidating by prospects who don't fancy themselves as "techies."

In short, Zapier uses technology to connect multiple tools
and services to one another, helping to automate otherwise
manual tasks. Let's say you're hosting a webinar to attract
leads; you could use Zapier to make sure that each person
who clicks on your Facebook ad is automatically registered
for the Zoom webinar, and that each new registrant to the
Zoom event is automatically added as a lead in Salesforce.

To make sure that potential customers can understand
how easy Zapier's service is to use and how compatible it is
with the services they already know and love, the company
has created a rich library of content that both **informs** and
coaches. For each compatible service (Facebook, Zoom,
and Salesforce in our previous example), Zapier has dedicated an entire page to educational content. There are
plenty of pages to choose from, but I'll use Zoom to illustrate the point.

The web page starts with a visual list of all the apps that
can be integrated with Zoom, including Google Calendar,
Slack, PayPal, and more. Beneath that is a section listing
popular app combinations, such as "Add new Zoom meetings to Google Calendar." Next comes a list of Zoom triggers
that can create actions in other apps ("When a new meeting is created...") and Zoom actions that can be triggered
by other apps ("... create webinar registrant.") The page
also lists similar tools you can explore integrations for (in
case, for example, you prefer GoToMeeting to Zoom). These
sections ensure that prospects are fully informed about the
role Zapier can play in helping them automate Zoom-related
tasks. This one page gives viewers a clear understanding of

what apps they can connect to Zoom, how others have made use of the integrations, and what specific tasks or actions they can automate.

In addition to all of this useful information about the integration, the page also has a coaching-oriented "Help" section that walks viewers through the more action-oriented aspects of using Zapier with Zoom. Here you'll find a "How to Get Started with Zoom on Zapier" document that gives an overview of the setup process step-by-step with screen-shots, as well as videos that offer visual walkthroughs of other integration processes.

Prospects now find themselves with few barriers to using Zapier: they know *what* they can do, and they have resources on *how* to do it.

This level of education doesn't exist just for Zoom. There's an equally helpful page for each of the more than 3,000 tools, platforms, and services that Zapier can be con-nected to. With so much educational content, any concerns about complexity and compatibility are almost entirely eliminated, and Zapier's claim to be "the easiest way to automate your work" becomes almost impossible to refute.

Exactly What to Do Now

BY PHIL M JONES

Now that you're armed with the six big lists you started in the previous chapter, it's time to put them to work. Your job is to prove your convenience—and now you have three focuses to help you build your case: corroboration, demonstration, and education.

So let's put your mind to work and get clear on the specific evidence of convenience you might be able to produce. This list of questions—and those you will find in all the chapters that follow—is by no means exhaustive. Think of these questions as guardrails that will guide you toward developing your own "Prove It" mentality, and that will help you "pre-purpose" your efforts in a way that puts at the center the needs and insecurities that affect the decision-making process of your customers.

- Can you link the speed of your service to someone or something that's locally accepted as being fast?

- What prompts could you put in place to ensure that more of your reviews reference your speed and ease of use?

- Is there a case study you could produce about a client who found you more convenient that your competitor?

- Do you have recent customers who might participate in a video testimonial about how easy it was to do business with you?

- Where do you need to answer convenience-related questions on your website?

- What one piece of content could you create to show future customers how your products and services integrate with others?

6

Proving Comparability

W HEN I WAS a kid, my parents used to take me to the
local flea market. On each trip, as we got out of the car
and walked toward the rows of booths, they'd hand
me a $5 bill to spend on whatever I wanted. When
you're six, having $5 is like having $5,000.

Most of those trips we made to the flea market have now
blended together in my memory, except for one. I remember
approaching a booth full of toys and beelining straight to the
section with the dolls. I was in my Barbie phase, and I could
spot those pink boxes a mile away. In front of the table was
a neon green poster with "$3" written on it in permanent
marker. I felt like I'd hit the jackpot, finding a secret stash
of dolls at a fraction of their store price.

But as I scanned the rows of glamorous blondes with
impossible proportions, sparkly outfits, and little plastic shoes,
my mom noticed that something was just a little bit . . . off.

"Are these real Barbies?" she asked the man behind the table.

"Pretty much," he said, shrugging.

"Pretty much" was good enough for me. My mom remained unconvinced and tried to tell me I'd be better off putting my $5 toward the Veterinarian Barbie I had seen on TV. Alas, I was six; delaying gratification wasn't really my strong suit.

As soon as we got to the car, I opened the box and took the doll out—obviously, I needed to brush her hair right away so she'd look her best when she met her new friends waiting at home. But before we even left the parking lot, her hollow blonde head popped off her neck and fell into my lap.

I don't remember this next part, but when my mom tells the story, she loves to imitate my reaction. She folds her arms across her chest and angrily says, "You know what you get when you buy a $3 Barbie, Mom? You *get* a $3 Barbie!"

Lesson learned: Just because something looks comparable doesn't mean it is.

You know that your products are not a cheap imitation of the competition or a lower-quality knock-off of another provider in your industry. But your competitors' products may be. And when faced with a number of choices that all seem "pretty much" the same, your consumers may decide they're OK with "pretty much" and go with someone other than you. This is why differentiating yourself by proving your comparability is so important. You want to ensure that your prospects have no doubt about which offering is the superior choice, long before they reach for their wallets. Generally speaking, when a business is using a comparability claim, they aren't just saying they're "pretty much" the same. Most often, comparability claims express some level of superiority over a specific competitor, or over their competitive set, putting them in a class of their own.

Creating content that proves your comparability is increasingly important, given how much information can be learned about product options with the swipe of a finger or click of a mouse. Studies have shown that 36% of consumers spend 30 minutes or more comparison shopping before making a purchase, and 65% spend at least 16 minutes on comparing their options. By creating content that serves as evidence of your comparability, you increase the chances that customers' comparison shopping will lead them to you.

Types of Comparability Claims

Comparability claims come in a few varieties, bucketed based on the factors that consumers tend to consider most when comparing available services and solutions. Claiming to be comparable means declaring how you measure up to the competition in terms of things like quality, durability, and affordability.

Quality claims are those that endorse the value of the solution you are providing, either on its own or in direct comparison to other available solutions. Claims like these speak to the caliber of your product and to the performance standards that your customers can expect.

Here are some real-life examples of comparability claims:

"Nothing runs like a Deere."—John Deere

"The best a man can get."—Gillette

"The ultimate driving machine."—BMW

Durability claims address a prospect's concerns about the longevity of the solutions you're offering, assuring them that your solution will continue to solve their problem for years to come, not just in the short term. (Had I known about the difference in the durability of the knock-off Barbie doll, for example, I might have heeded my mom's advice.)

Here are some real-life examples of durability claims:

"It keeps going... and going... and going."—Energizer

"Takes a licking and keeps on ticking."—Timex

"Stop dieting. Get lifelong results."—Noom

Affordability claims are those that place a stake in the ground with regards to price or the value they deliver. Businesses making these claims often emphasize the financial accessibility of their products or services in comparison to others, but they may also claim that their competitors are inflating their prices or otherwise charging more than they should.

Here are some real-life examples of affordability claims:

"Everyday low prices."—Walmart

"Low fares. Nothing to hide. That's TransFarency!"
—Southwest Airlines

"High quality training that's affordable and convenient."
—Lynda.com

Some companies—like Payless, Dollar Tree, and Five Below—even work their affordability claim right into their names.

You may think that having the cheapest price means you're guaranteed to win in a comparison with your competition, but that's not the only factor consumers consider. For many of them, it's not even the most important.

Proving Comparability with Corroboration

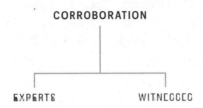

Comparability is most easily proven by corroboration, since companies and products are so routinely ranked, certified, and awarded by industry authorities. Subaru does a fantastic job of translating their awards into evidence, with an entire page of their site dedicated to sharing ratings and rankings compiled by third-party **experts**.

To prove how long-lasting and reliable their vehicles are compared to others, Subaru shares an Experian study of vehicle registrations showing that in 2022, 96% of Subarus sold in the last 10 years are still on the road today. To prove how well their vehicles perform compared to others, they note that Kelley Blue Book—the leading auto industry authority on vehicle pricing and value—crowned them "Best Performance Brand" not once but five times. And, to prove how safe their vehicles are compared to those from other manufacturers, Subaru shares that the Insurance Institute for Highway Safety gave the highest possible rating for front crash prevention to all 2021 Subaru models with the EyeSight system. Plus, if you wanted proof from witnesses—delivered by experts—you'd see that the American Customer Satisfaction Index rated Subaru #1 in vehicle safety too.

But the claim that Subaru backs up with the most proof has to do with how loved they are by their customers—the **witnesses**. Kelley Blue Book is cited again, having named Subaru their "Most Trusted Brand" for seven years running, and awarding them "Best Overall Brand" four times, based on consumer beliefs about the brand. J.D. Power & Associates also makes an appearance as an expert here, declaring Subaru as having the "#1 Brand Loyalty" in the automotive industry for two years in a row, based on how loyal Subaru customers are.

Subaru is in the lucky position to have been ranked so highly by multiple different industry authorities, but you don't need a heaping pile of awards to prove your comparability. Appearing on a local publication's "best of" list is equally worthy of celebration and elevation through content. Content that demonstrates your own customers' stories (such as the examples that follow in the next section) can also provide powerful comparative proof when they detail what those customers have tried before—without success—before discovering your solution. You can even encourage your customers to talk about how you compare to other brands they have tried in their reviews and testimonials.

Proving Comparability with Demonstration

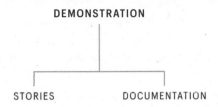

Many businesses use some version of the customer success story to demonstrate their comparability. That's because these stories take their comparability claims and place them firmly in the real world, in the context of a real person that consumers can relate to.

These **stories**—whether they come in the form of an article, a video, or something else—tend to follow a similar progression. The story starts by setting the stage by introducing the characters and helping the audience understand the situation. Next comes the challenge, or the problem that needed to be solved. Typically this section would be followed by the story of finding and using your solution, but if the aim is to prove comparability, ideally that will be preceded by an account of a *failed* attempt to solve the problem with a competitive "solution."

The customer might share how their previous realtor failed to sell their home for months, how their pup chewed through every other toy they had bought, or how their last regimen was just too expensive for the minimal results it created. And then—right when the customer was at their most frustrated, disappointed, and hopeless—your solution arrived. Your offering helped them achieve the results they had been dreaming of, and you all lived happily ever after.

The "happily ever after" might be a stretch, but that's the sort of triumphant ending you're going for when you use a customer success story to prove comparability. You want to demonstrate that while a prospect looking at your offerings may have tried *many* things, they haven't tried *your* thing, and they just might get the results they've been hoping for with you.

Infomercials are great inspiration when it comes to using **documentation** to prove comparability. No infomercial is complete without the side-by-side comparison of the star product and the lowly competitor that inevitably absorbs less, lifts less, moves slower, or otherwise just doesn't get the job done. Whether it's two cleaners being used on the same stain, two cosmetics applied to the same face, or two tools attempting the same repair, these demonstrations aim to prove that *looking* similar and *performing* similar are not the same thing.

That said, infomercials can also have a flair for the dramatic. (I'm looking at you, black-and-white scene of someone being buried in plastic container lids, spilling an entire bowl of pasta sauce on a white shirt, or stepping into a bucket of dirty water while mopping the floor.) With your documentation, you'll likely want to take an approach that's a bit more realistic so you don't undermine the importance of the problem you're solving or make your solution (and brand) feel like a gimmick.

It's worth noting that this type of demonstration can also happen in-store or live at a trade show booth. Live demonstrations allow for a more immersive experience, giving your prospects the chance to see, feel, hear, smell, or taste the difference themselves. And if you can capture those authentic reactions to a comparison on video, you can amplify the impact of your demo when you share it with prospects who can't be there themselves.

Proving Comparability with Education

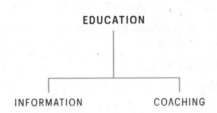

Providing evidence that educates your prospects is especially important when your product or service is technical in nature, or otherwise difficult for a layperson to compare on their own. It won't be effective to rattle off a series of stats and specs as proof of how you compare if your audience doesn't understand what those numbers represent.

Sometimes, in order to make that comparison easy to understand, you're going to need to offer **informational content** about your competitors. This is especially true if your solutions cost more than others'. You'll likely need to create content that informs your audience about how your pricing is set, what factors affect price, and what features or benefits the cheaper solutions *don't* offer. While it might seem strange to talk about your competitors' solutions if they're priced cheaper, 78% of consumers say they are likely to return to a retailer who shows competitors' prices.

In the late 2000s, Apple ran a series of commercials that you might remember as the "I'm a Mac, I'm a PC" ads. Every ad featured the same two people—each representing one of the device types—engaged in playful banter that always ended up with the Mac character displaying better quality, more practicality, superior design, and so on. In one of the ads, for example, Mac and PC are attempting to discuss their similarities, but PC keeps freezing and "restarting." In another, PC appears wearing a full biohazard suit, warning of the dangers of viruses before telling a casually dressed Mac that he's lucky he doesn't have to deal with viruses. Another spot features Mac politely declining a disguise that PC is using to hide from spyware.

In perhaps the most cutting spot, PC introduces himself as "an incredibly easy-to-use PC," and some fine print appears at the bottom of the screen. "Just a little legal copy," he says, dismissing it. As the commercial goes on, more legal copy appears on screen with each positive claim the PC makes. (Mac's claims receive no such treatment.) By the end of the 30-second spot, the screen is completely covered by lines of legal copy.

Without even choosing a specific point of comparison, Apple has **coached** its potential buyers to understand that, even if their competitors claim to be comparable to a Mac, consumers will need to look a bit closer to see the truth.

Sometimes, though, you'll need to educate your audience about a process—rather than facts—to show how you compare.

One of my favorite examples of coaching consumers through a process that demonstrates comparability comes from Jim's Automotive Machine Shop in Gill, Colorado. The shop is run by a father-son pair: Jimmie Wolfrum started the shop in 1983, and his son Nicolaus built a thriving secondary business selling parts on eBay. Their YouTube channel boasts more than 260,000 subscribers. Those are some impressive numbers for a small-town machine shop "specializing in light industrial and agricultural engine machine work."

In one nearly 20-minute video—titled "How do WE clean YOUR engine parts in our machine shop?" on YouTube—Nicolaus walks viewers through each of the steps in the detailed process the shop uses to clean grease- and rust-covered engine blocks thoroughly, until they look brand new again. He tours the shop showing each machine they use, sharing how it works, and listing the pros and cons of each product or approach. There's plenty of detail and lots of side-by-side engine blocks shown to demonstrate effectiveness.

Around the halfway mark, Nicolaus acknowledges that the process they use at their shop takes a lot longer than others' and that it's a lot more work: "A lot of shops . . . they don't want to take the time because it doesn't pay as well as just running it through the spray cabinet and calling it good," he explains. "But it's a better product, it keeps our shop cleaner, and it makes the customer happier. That's why we take the time to do it."

The comments on the video are evidence of how well this coaching content has worked to distinguish the shop from its competitors:

- "I have had several blocks prepped by a few different machine shops here in Texas, and NONE have been cleaned this well by a long shot!!"

- "The machine shop we use definitely did not get stuff that clean."

- "I wish the shop I work at was as clean as y'all's."

- "I know who I'm sending blocks to now!"

By creating this content, Jim's Automotive has managed to educate viewers on how they compare to other local shops, as well as on how their customers are the envy of others spread across the country:

- "Wish my local machinist would clean my blocks that good."

- "I wish you guys were a little closer but it might be worth the trip to get better work."

- "I live in TX and would almost drive to CO just to have my stuff done in your shop."

But my favorite comment on the video came from Vincent G:

> I'm not saying we are better, I'm giving you the proof that we are better ;) In my opinion, this is one of the best forms of advertising. You can yell slogans all day, but if your customers know that you are doing good work, this is the best advertisement you can get.

How's that for proof of the effectiveness of proof? Completely organically, Jim's has inspired a viewer to acknowledge how well this educational content worked to prove the comparably superior workmanship of the shop and to praise the team for using the tactic.

Exactly What to Do Now

BY PHIL M JONES

Your head is now likely spinning with powerful ideas for proving how your product's strengths compare to the alternatives. But what practical steps can you take to actually start moving your case of evidence forward?

Perhaps the answers to these questions may get you well on your way:

- Who could you collaborate with to produce an "us versus them" comparison piece that lives somewhere more impartial than your own website?

- How could you create an honest comparison challenge—like a blind taste test—and document it for your future customers?

- Could you produce a case study of one of your customers who historically favored a competitor's product and is now delighted to have found you as an alternative?

- What side-by-side images or infographics do you need to create to show your differences?

- What kind of blog posts could you produce to answer in detail why you are different from each major competitor?

- What type of "how to" videos could you create that would also work to demonstrate your superiority to your competitors?

7

Proving Commitment

N EARLY 2021, my daughter was diagnosed with a nut
allergy. Since then, my grocery trips have taken quite a
bit longer, as everything that makes its way into my cart
now needs to be carefully scrutinized to rule out the pres
ence of nuts or traces.

A few places need to be checked in order for me to
screen out potentially dangerous foods. Sometimes potential allergens are marked in bold within the packaging's
ingredients list: olive oil, **cashews**, salt... Allergens may
also be highlighted underneath the ingredients list with a
warning: *Contains Peanuts* or *May Contain Traces of Almonds*.
The sneakiest one to look out for is the manufacturing
note, which discloses that a product was produced with
equipment that also processes one or more of the common
allergens: *Produced in a facility that also processes tree nuts*.

Even familiar products need to be checked for confir-
mation each time they're grabbed off the shelf. "New Look,

Same Great Taste" could mean there's been a recipe change, and while the last package of crackers may have been produced in a nut-free facility, that doesn't mean that this month's shipment came from the same location.

This process is as time-consuming as it is stressful. The stakes are high. I often double-check and triple-check the labels before checkout to be sure I haven't missed something. And I'd be lying if I said I didn't check packaging again before serving food at home ... just in case.

But the truth is, no matter how diligently I check labels, my daughter's safety is ultimately contingent upon the truthfulness and transparency of the companies we buy from. I have to trust that manufacturers are being honest about the ingredients they use, the facilities in which their products are manufactured, and the other ingredients being processed with their machinery. I need to believe they are as committed to disclosing allergen information as I am to looking for it, and as committed to protecting their customers as I am to protecting my child.

Every time I place my daughter's epinephrine injector in my bag, I'm reminded just how tenuous this whole system is. We've been lucky. To date, none of the products that passed the grocery-store check have gone on to cause a reaction bad enough to need the injector. But if you ask most parents of a child with serious food allergies, you'll hear stories about "safe" items that have caused anything from a few hives to full-on anaphylaxis.

It's not just parents of kids with allergies who rely on businesses doing the right thing. We all want to be assured that the businesses we give our money to are committed to the things they say they are—that they will protect us and live up to the values they claim to uphold.

Types of Commitment Claims

Claiming to be committed means insisting that you are worthy of trust and that you operate ethically, transparently, and fairly.

At the most basic level, most consumers expect a commitment to customer service. They expect companies to treat them with kindness and respect and to provide them with fair pricing. They expect a safe experience and environment, and to have any issues resolved quickly and fairly. They want to know that a business is committed to their satisfaction and will protect their property.

But consumers also trust that their financial institutions, healthcare providers, and all of the other organizations to whom they entrust their private data will protect that data. Or, they *want* to trust them, anyway: 84% of UK consumers say they wish they could trust more companies with their data. Many consumers also want to know that the companies they buy from are committed to hiring a diverse workforce and providing those employees with a living wage, a safe working environment, and humane treatment.

Some commitment claims relate to a businesses' **commitment to consumers**, emphasizing the way they prioritize the consumer over other business interests or the special care they take to ensure customer happiness. Here are some real-life examples of claims asserting a commitment to consumers:

> "You're in good hands."—Allstate

> "We try harder."—Avis

> "Nationwide is on your side."—Nationwide

> "We are ladies and gentlemen serving ladies and gentlemen."—Ritz-Carlton Hotel Company

Many consumers—particularly younger consumers—prefer to buy from companies that maintain a **commitment to values** they share and causes that matter to them: sustainability, diversity, gender equality, human rights, animal rights, and more. Studies have shown that 71% of consumers prefer to buy from brands that align with their values. What sort of values matter most? Well, 79% of global consumers prioritize brands that have fair and responsible behavior when buying materials, products, or services, and 78% said they prioritize brands that put customer interests ahead of profit. Another 71% preferred to shop with brands that are working to reduce their environmental impact.

Here are some real-life examples of claims relating to value commitment:

> "We're in business to save our home planet."—Patagonia

> "More fashion choices that are good for people, the planet, and your wallet."—H&M

> "To inspire and nurture the human spirit—one person, one cup, and one neighborhood at a time."—Starbucks

These types of value commitments are often linked to company purpose, meaning they are values held year-round and year after year. But many companies also make *temporary* claims associated with time-constrained causes. A great example of this is a company that makes a promise to donate a portion of sales to cancer research during

Breast Cancer Awareness Month. This is called "cause-related marketing," and consumers will often need to see even more proof of these more short-term value claims. A study published in the *International Journal of Business and Social Science* showed that, since these values seem to "come and go" based on the calendar, consumers want to be reassured that a company's actions are "cause-beneficial" and not just "cause-exploitative."

Translation: Your actions, priorities, and donation record need to show that you truly support a cause you are linking yourself to even outside of the times when it's popular to do so. If your commitment to, say, the cause of LGBTQ+ rights begins and ends with a rainbow logo on your site during Pride Month, your customers and prospects may see that logo as a hollow attempt to drive up sales.

Skepticism of these types of claims and behaviors among consumers is justified. In January 2021, the European Commission released a report showing that in 42% of cases in which companies were making some sort of "green" claim, those claims were "exaggerated, false, or deceptive." On top of that, more than 50% of companies didn't provide "sufficient information for consumers to judge the claim's accuracy," and nearly 60% didn't provide "easily accessible evidence to support its claim."

Making commitment claims that aren't backed up by actions is what marketing speaker Katie Martell calls "performative allyship," and—spoiler alert—this type of deceptive pandering rarely ends well for the brands that do it.

Proving Commitment with Corroboration

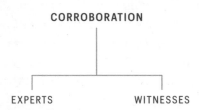

Given the high amount of skepticism regarding commitment claims, it shouldn't come as much of a surprise to learn that 70% of consumers say they are more likely to buy from a consumer products company that is "verified by a third party as having the highest standards of data privacy and security." As a result, commitment claims will often rely heavily on content that provides **expert corroboration**.

In the previous chapter, I pointed to Subaru as an example of a company that shares all of their awards to prove their comparability and competitiveness. Awards, rankings, and certifications like these can also play an important role in proving your commitment.

Want to prove your commitment to reducing your impact on the environment? Check out the World Sustainability Awards. Packaging Europe even gives out awards for sustainability in product packaging specifically.

Want to prove how committed you are to taking care of your employees? Companies like *Fortune*, Glassdoor, *Inc.*, Indeed, and Comparably give out annual awards (or compile annual lists) honoring the "Best Places to Work." Gallup has its Exceptional Workplace Award, and ClearlyRated gives out Employee Satisfaction awards.

Want to prove that you're committed to equality and diversity in the workplace? Crain's now gives out Excellence in Diversity and Inclusion awards, and the Catalyst Award celebrates organizations that drive representation and inclusion for women. *Fortune* acknowledges the 100 best workplaces for diversity.

You can also look into industry-specific awards that can do double-duty by both setting you apart from your competition and proving your commitment. For example, why go for a general run-of-the-mill sustainability award that covers all sectors if you can be acknowledged by your own industry's leading authority, like the Sustainability Awards from US Dairy? Don't forget to also look for local awards and rankings, which are likely to be more affordable than national or global awards (if there are application fees at all) and which offer a smaller application pool. Local or regional magazines and newspapers often give out a variety of "best of" awards acknowledging restaurants, bars, hotels, and other places worth visiting.

Of course, simply winning an award or making a list may not be enough proof on its own. It's your job to create content that celebrates that achievement in a way that makes it visible and obvious to your audience. There are plenty of ways to do it, but here are a few:

* Hang the certificates.

* Frame the magazine write-up.

* Put the "best of" sticker in your front window.

* Write and distribute a press release.

- Write a blog post praising all of the employees and departments who made the win possible.

- Document the awards ceremony with a video.

- Interview employees and customers about what this award means for them.

Many awards and rankings are given based on employee or customer ratings, which makes them a bit of a hybrid, providing expert as well as **witness corroboration**. Additionally, your employees can serve as witnesses for your commitment claims when they are the beneficiaries of the commitments. If you've made a commitment to supporting your associates' pursuit of higher education, have some employees share their experience of completing or pursuing a degree thanks to your support. If you've committed to flexible working conditions that allow caregivers or those with disabilities to maintain their employment, have those employees talk about what that accommodation has meant for them.

It's important to note, though, that employees are best used as witnesses specifically for content about those commitments from which they directly benefit. Having employees vouch for other types of commitments—a focus on sustainability, for example—may not be perceived as genuine; they may end up coming across as just another "company mouthpiece" sharing some pre-determined talking points.

Proving Commitment with Demonstration

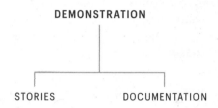

As you begin to look for ways to prove your own commitment through **stories** and **documentation**, you can look to non-profit organizations for inspiration. Many charities and cause-related organizations use "impact stories" to help demonstrate the difference their efforts are making. For example, wildlife organizations and shelters often share heart-wrenching stories of an animal's abuse, neglect, or injury, and then document the dedicated employees or volunteers who are working tirelessly to nurse the creature back to its happy, healthy, and adorable self. Stories like these not only prove how committed these organizations are to their cause but also make a great case for continued support of those efforts.

Your stories needn't be as dramatic as a beached whale rescue documented in high-definition video. Any content that documents you, your team, or your organization living out your values can serve as evidence to back up your commitment claims. You might share a photo on social media of your team volunteering together, packaging donations, or marching in a parade or protest. You could upload a video to your website of your executives delivering a check (giant *or* regular sized) to an organization you support. And, of course, you can display the certificates and inspection reports that show you've lived up to the standards you promise. Hang that "A" rating from the health inspector proudly.

One way to use documentation to prove your commitment is to share company reports, assessments, scores, or other data that would normally be kept private. (Assuming, of course, that this data demonstrates your commitment and that sharing it doesn't violate any laws or privacy policies.) Buffer—a social media publishing tool—firmly believes in pay equity and transparency. "We're committed to providing fair and competitive compensation," the company says on its site. But Buffer also goes beyond saying it—the team actually demonstrates this commitment at buffer.com/salaries, where they publicly share every single employee's annual pay, alongside their name, department, job title, and location. By sharing this information, which would normally be kept under wraps, Buffer is walking its talk about being committed to pay transparency. With all that salary information documented and easily accessible, the company is not only holding itself accountable publicly, but it's also making it easier for applicants to enter pay conversations armed with all the information they need to feel confident they're being treated fairly.

What makes this move even more impressive is that it's actually pretty rare for companies that make these types of pay equity commitments to share evidence. In a JUST Capital poll of company wages and workplace inclusivity from 2016, for example, only 65 of the 890 companies evaluated disclosed the results of any analysis they had conducted on their gender pay gap, and only 126 had done such an evaluation in the first place.

If you're able to find ways to document your commitment by sharing data evidence like this, you have a huge opportunity to not just prove the truth of your commitment but actually set yourself apart from countless others who aren't willing or able to bring similar evidence.

Proving Commitment with Education

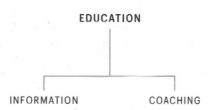

EDUCATION

INFORMATION   COACHING

Proving commitment is often done with **informational content** that gives your audience insight into the commitment you're making. This type of content explains the context of the commitment, its importance, and what this commitment *really* means.

Here are some kinds of information that might be valuable to include or cover in this type of content:

- What this commitment means
- What this commitment does *not* mean
- What making this commitment entails
- Why this commitment is important
- What happens without this commitment
- How to know if someone is truly making this commitment

Informational content is especially important for companies with a complex or technical offering, as your audience may not understand the relevance of your distinguishing commitment. For example, if you claim to be committed to producing your products without palm oil, your audience may not fully appreciate the meaning of this claim. Since 66% of consumers say they are attracted to brands that are transparent about where materials are sourced, you'll want to be sure to contextualize these claims accordingly—say, by informing your audience about how harvesting palm oil contributes to deforestation.

If your company collects private personal information from consumers and has a privacy policy to match, you're not off the hook. On average, only 13% of consumers completely read the privacy protection policy. Simply *having* a policy is not enough. You have to create informational content—in easily understood language—that clearly informs customers of the commitment you're making to protecting their personal data.

Another approach to informational content is to explain the rationale behind a commitment through the lens of opinion or with a first-person narrative detailing the importance of the commitment. In cases where a founder or leader has a public presence and is vocal about their background and inspiration, sharing that story can be both informative and relatable. A great example of this is TOMS Shoes, a company initially founded with the mission of donating one pair of shoes for each pair purchased. The company hints at this origin story on its "About" page:

> While traveling through Argentina in 2006, TOMS founder Blake Mycoskie saw the hardships faced by

children without shoes. This inspired him to create a for-profit business with giving at its core. The idea? For every pair of shoes the company sold, a new pair would be given to a child in need.

While this page explains the company's purpose—their "what"—it doesn't quite give us enough details or context to deeply understand the "why."

By contrast, here's a snippet from a 2011 piece for *Entrepreneur*, where Blake Mycoskie shared a more in-depth first-person description of his experience in Argentina:

> It was heartbreaking... It dramatically heightened my awareness. Yes, I knew somewhere in the back of my mind that poor children around the world often went barefoot, but now, for the first time, I saw the real effects of being shoeless: the blisters, the sores, the infections. I wanted to do something about it. But what?

This first-person approach is more emotional and visceral: it puts us inside the TOMS founder's head and gives us a much clearer picture of the importance of this mission. The "buy one, give one" model that TOMS was founded on was not just about making some feel-good donations. We can now see why that issue was so important to Blake and the degree to which his model helped children who received the donated shoes.

Since 65% of global consumers think CEOs should be accountable to the public and not just to their board or their stockholders, this approach to providing context for commitment with a leader's own narrative can be particularly effective. Walking consumers through a process with

coaching content can also help demystify the processes used to maintain your commitments.

Any entities that collect customers' personal information should create educational content that shows the steps they take to protect that data. Almost three-quarters of consumers say that a more easily understandable privacy policy would increase their trust in a consumer product company, and 80% agree that both clearly stating how consumer data will be used each time data is collected *and* asking for consent would also increase their trust. By walking your customers through how their data is collected, stored, and protected, you can increase their understanding, and thereby their trust. The level of detail that you share about your data protection processes and policies—and the fact that you've taken the time to share it at all—will help consumers see that your commitment to maintaining their privacy is genuine.

Exactly What to Do Now

BY PHIL M JONES

My guess is that you and your clients have a lot of commitments. Taking the time to methodically focus on proving these commitments is a commitment in itself. Get crystal clear on your own commitments to start shaping your action plan for proving them. Begin by answering these questions:

- Who is an external ambassador you could partner with to prove your commitment to your values or cause?

- Instead of stating how long you've been doing something, how could you translate that claim to an actual number or statistic, such as how many people you have helped, what resources you have invested, or how much of an impact you have made?

- Could you work with your employees to produce evidence for the contributions you make to the community as a whole?

- When did you last review all of the imagery you use in your marketing to ensure it represents your chosen position on diversity?

- How can you change the positioning of all "about us" content away from what you do, and toward why you do it, how you do it, and who you do it for?

- What content needs to exist in your employee onboarding experience that could coach their competence on the "why" behind your organization's "what"?

8

Proving
Connection

I N 1997, my mom was in the market for a new car. Having had a negative experience with a male salesperson in the past, she decided she wanted a female representative this time around. She found Catherine Reed at Shaker's Family Ford Lincoln in Watertown, Connecticut, and hoped she'd get the family experience that the company promised.

Cathy sold us an "Atlantic blue" Ford Escort. My mom got her first birthday card from Cathy later that year, and when the new year rolled around, Cathy sent us a 1998 calendar featuring a photo taken of us standing next to the Escort on "Purchase Day." We even got a "cariversary" card in the mail one year after we first walked into the dealership.

Cathy treated us like family.

Five years later, Cathy helped my mom replace the Escort with an Escape, and as the number of drivers in our family grew, she helped us add a bright blue Focus to the mix. When my first car (not a Ford) died three days before I was set to drive seven hours to my summer internship, guess who we called? Within a day, Cathy had found my mom a new car she loved so I could take the Focus to my internship for the summer. That alone would have been great, but while we were inside the dealership signing the paperwork, she also had our Focus detailed so that I would get to have that "new car" feeling too.

Cathy goes above and beyond, not just for us, but for all her clients. I was unsurprised to see that she has so many positive reviews on DealerRater.com. Most of the reviews mention the wonderful experience Cathy provides, but there are also a few exceptional ones that speak to the way she fulfills the "Family" promise:

- "I arrived at the dealership to look at the vehicle with a sleeping toddler and a newborn. Cathy ran back and forth from her desk to my car to work out the purchase information."

- "Cathy called us several times to update us during the week prior to our pick up date."

- "Cathy Reed... made me a personalized video of the vehicle and sent it to me prior to my visit."

Building that type of connection is what creates lifelong customers. Between our immediate family and all the relatives and friends we've referred to Cathy, we know of at least nine cars that have been purchased from her because of the family experience we got in that first interaction in 1997. And we're not alone. Here are a few more snippets from reviews of Cathy Reed's service:

- "This is my 3rd purchase with Cathy Reed."

- "This is my 4th vehicle from Shaker's and with Cathy's assistance. That really says it all. I recommend Cathy and Shaker's to everyone."

- "Cathy Reed is simply the best. She has been our car adviser for nearly 30 years now and we plan on going back to her for the rest of our lives. Enough said. I can't think of a better testimonial than that!"

But not everyone is going to have a friend of a friend to tell them about your incredible service, and not everyone will be willing to scroll through hundreds of reviews to see how much you care about your customers. That's why providing evidence of your connectedness is key.

Types of Connection Claims

Claiming to be connected makes the promise that you prioritize close relationships. These claims relate to loyalty, your role in the community, your independent operations, and your closeness with your customers, vendors, or others. Most connection claims refer specifically to **personal relationships**, aiming to assure your audience that you as a company maintain a close bond and deep sense of caring for your individual customers. And this more human business claim is increasingly important for consumers.

New technology tools are tantalizing and sometimes necessary, but the human touch remains enormously important. Today, 64% of US consumers and 59% of all consumers feel companies have lost touch with the human element of customer experience. 71% of Americans would rather interact with a human than a chatbot or some other automated process. (Tom Puthiyamadam and José Reyes, PricewaterhouseCoopers)

These types of claims are especially common with local, family-owned, and independent businesses, where the personal nature of service can be a significant differentiator from national brands or big-box providers. Here are some real-life examples of claims that assert an emphasis on personal relationships:

> "Where you're a name, not a number."—Oklahoma City University

> "Large enough to serve you, small enough to know you." —Hampton Roads Educators Credit Union

> "When you're here, you're family."—Olive Garden

Other commitment claims are focused on connection with **the local community**. This form of commitment often plays out with company policies that encourage, support, or even mandate contributions to the business's community. These claims are often closely related to values-based commitment claims but have an express focus on local communities and organizations. Community commitment claims can include things like

- annual allowances for paid time off to volunteer with local organizations;

- in-store donation collection of food, clothing, school supplies, and more;

- support for local clean-up projects or natural disaster relief;

- free or discounted products and services for local nonprofits; and

- nomination of local organizations for corporate support or grants.

Many large corporations and franchises have company-wide programs that ensure leftover food isn't wasted and is instead donated to local homeless shelters, soup kitchens, and other organizations fighting food insecurity in their community. Panera Bread's "Day-End Dough-Nation" program redistributes any baked goods left at the end of the day to local non-profits, and Starbucks' FoodShare program has been minimizing food waste by donating leftover food since 2016.

Here are some real-life examples of claims that assert an emphasis on connection to the community:

"Providing community and good food for all, regardless of means."—A Place at the Table

"Like a good neighbor, State Farm is there."—State Farm

"Locally strong."—True Value Hardware

Proving Connection with Corroboration

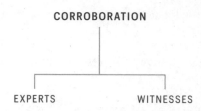

The 2021 *Edelman Trust Barometer* showed that consumers are more trusting of scientists than any other source. This is actually a form of **expert corroboration**, and their perspective can go a long way toward validating the importance of any connection claims you make.

This is a great time to bring to light and amplify any awards that speak to your connection, particularly awards that relate to things like community excellence, customer satisfaction, employee satisfaction, customer experience, customer service, customer loyalty, and similar honors.

Beyond awards, you're bound to be able to find experts in your field who can share the importance of a business having a deep connection with customers, employees, partners, or the community. For example, if your company uses or sells a variety of locally sourced goods, you can find plenty of experts—human or data—to underscore how supporting local businesses helps both the local economy and the environment. Add in the expert perspective of one of your suppliers on top of that as a way to validate and personalize the more general data, and you've built a case for the positive impact your specific connection is having.

Take this example: If you're in the healthcare space and you're looking to back up a claim about how deeply your staff cares for patients, you can cite data that shows the positive impact a doctor-patient relationship has on health outcomes. Pairing that with insight from a trusted local medical expert—perhaps some of the specialists you refer patients to—would validate and underscore the importance of the extra connection you and your staff have with the people in your care.

Speaking of the people in your care, some of the best evidence of your connection is going to come in the form of **witness testimonials**. Think back to my example of our favorite car salesperson Cathy and her rave reviews on DealerRater.com. In fact, that same *Edelman Trust Barometer* that ranked scientists as the most trusted sources also showed that consumers are more likely to trust "people in my local community" than government leaders, religious leaders, journalists, and CEOs.

Ideally, if you're offering top-notch customer service and genuinely connecting with your customers, some of this will shine through in the reviews or testimonials being left organically. But that doesn't mean you should just wait and hope. Take advantage of any opportunities you have to keep in touch with your audience, and use those communications to explicitly ask for reviews and testimonials that can serve as proof of your connection. You can take a cue from the restaurant and retail industries by placing a call to action for reviews at the bottom of your receipts, for example.

You might also send this kind of request in a follow-up email after a positive interaction. Data shows that up to 80% of reviews come from these types of follow-up emails that ask customers to review a purchase. This is something I have done as a speaker for years, and it has allowed me to create a robust directory of reviews and testimonials that affirm my connection with audiences during events, and with my hosts prior. After any positive email from an event organizer, keynote attendee, or workshop participant, I reply asking if they'd be open to me sharing their experience in a testimonial.

When you're specifically looking to build evidence of connection, use prompts that will encourage reviews with that type of information. For example, you might ask a contact to share insight on whether they felt listened to, if their experience was personalized, if the interaction was pleasant, and if your advice and guidance showed a deep understanding of their needs and challenges.

Proving Connection with Demonstration

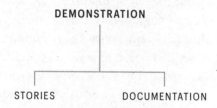

We've discussed the ways that content showing customer success stories can be used to prove comparability, but you can take a similar approach to show your connectedness too. You just need to shift your focus: rather than emphasizing success with your offering, these specific stories are strictly about the customer.

Customer **stories** are entirely about the person: their background, achievements, beliefs, hobbies, loved ones, and more. When creating this type of content, choose people with whom your business has a longstanding relationship, a unique bond, or some other exceptional connection. You might share the story of the customer who has been coming to your cafe to read the morning paper every day for 25 years, or detail the love story of the couple who got engaged at your fitness center. You may even just have small "customer spotlights" on social media or in your newsletter that give your regulars a moment to shine.

This approach—sharing stories about people with whom you are connected—doesn't need to be limited to customer stories, either. You can create content that shows your deep bond with employees, neighbors, vendors, community leaders, partners, or any other person or group. You might tell the story of the family who has had three generations employed at your shop, the concierge at your hotel who knows the town better than anyone else, the farmer who provides the local vegetables on your menu, or the charity you co-hosted an event with.

By creating content about these individuals, you're signaling to your customers—past, present, and potential—that you care deeply about people. Depending on the types of stories you tell and the relationships you focus on, this content may also be doing double-duty by providing evidence of your commitment to a particular value or cause, as well as your connection.

The "Stories" section of the Starbucks website is full of feel-good content detailing the commitment of the company and its partners in supporting their communities and the people within it:

- "Starbucks manager and barista join forces to help get money for free health clinic."

- "A Shanghai barista leads Starbucks partners, customers to volunteer with kids each month."

- "Store manager brings COVID-19 supplies to Navajo Nation."

- "Starbucks customers, partners help Maui food bank meet growing need."

- "Starbucks in Indonesia brings coffee to nurses and front-line workers."

- "Starbucks murals become first 'blossom' in a neighbor-hood rebuilding."

Documentation can also show your connection—and some of the best documentation for connection claims can be found in an unexpected place. If you set foot into a locally owned pizza parlor or sandwich shop, you'll almost always find certificates on the walls thanking the owners for their support of a local kids' sports team. Often it's a baseball or football team, but it could be a competitive cheerleading squad, a youth soccer team, or the local swimming and diving league. You won't have to look too far to find out: nearby, you'll likely find a team photo—proudly framed and prominently hung—featuring rows of pint-sized athletes smiling in their uniforms.

This kind of sponsorship is about more than having "Stella's Pizza" screen-printed on a jersey as advertising. It means offering a free slice to the kid who scores the winning goal and helping the whole team celebrate with a pizza party at the end of the season, win or lose. It conveys that you are a member of the community who is so proud to be supporting a generation of athletes you've watched grow up that you've cut out newspaper coverage of their wins and taped the clippings up on the wall.

You'd be hard-pressed to find better proof—better documentation—of your connection to your community than those framed team photos next to the register.

Proving Connection with Education

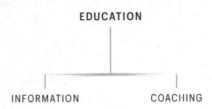

As with other types of claims, connection claims often need to be contextualized to help the audience fully understand them.

Want to make sure that your audience understands the importance of your ingredients or products being sourced locally from a farmer you know and trust? Create **informational content** that walks them through the difference that it makes in your local economy. This type of content not only shows your connection to your community, but it also encourages their ongoing support of that connection, since 57% of Americans say their main reason for shopping small is to keep money local.

Want to emphasize the importance of your annual school supply drive and the impact it has on local schoolchildren? Don't just create content that shares the amount of school supplies your team has donated over the years. To increase the impact of your evidence, also provide additional information that helps educate your audience about why that connection matters. You might share that the average American family spends over $1,000 per child each year on school supplies, extracurricular fees, and technology, and that 94% of American public school teachers spend their own money on needed supplies for their classrooms, without getting reimbursed. You might address the depth of the need in your community by referring to unemployment statistics or the percentage of local children who qualify for reduced lunch prices. With this type of added context, your connection to the school and the difference you make with your supply drive is suddenly clearer.

More personal, opinion-style content also has a role in proving connection, allowing you to inform your audience of the reasons why you prioritize building and maintaining connections. Talk about the customers who have made a lasting impact on you, or the experiences that inspired you to place such a high value on connections.

In case you didn't notice, this is exactly what I've been doing in the introduction to each chapter in this half of the book: I've shared a personal experience that shows why I value this particular type of claim. With each chapter, I am making my own claim that this type of evidence matters and makes a difference in the decision-making process of your customer, and these stories have been my way of backing that claim up.

At the risk of creating an *Inception*-type situation here... content like this, which teaches your audience more about you, not only serves as proof of your connections but also allows that audience to relate to you better, which can create a deeper connection with them—helping your proof drive your claim.

While most of the educational content you create as evidence of connection will likely be informational, you can do this with **coaching content** too. Remember Jim's Automotive Machine Shop from a couple chapters earlier? They're the ones who proved their comparability with a video showing the more detailed and time-consuming way that they clean engine blocks, compared to other shops. You could take a similar approach to creating evidence of your connection too. Coming back to that school supply drive example, you might also create a detailed video showing how your team assembles the supply-filled backpacks to donate, arming your audience with the knowledge to be able to do the same for a school that's near and dear to their own hearts. You might walk through the detailed process by which you select the beneficiaries of your corporate social responsibility initiatives, showing what you consider and how you decide. You could also create content that goes through the steps your sales team takes to gather and keep track of important client data—like birthdays, anniversaries, or favorite sports teams—enabling them to build a relationship beyond the sale.

Exactly What to Do Now

BY PHIL M JONES

Proving your connection is about creating objective evidence to support a subjective outcome. There is a lot you can do to amplify this outcome, but first consider how easy it can be to lose your connection to your audience if you forget how important it is to people to feel valued at the right level.

Before you start building any new evidence, review the risks in your process that might lose you trust. The trend toward automated communications can sabotage relationships more than enhance them, since you are losing the ability to show that you remember people's names, key dates, and the specifics of their relationship to you.

To quote relationship expert John Ruhlin, "It's not the thought that counts, it's the thoughtful thought that counts." Here are some questions to help guide that thoughtful thought:

- How can you enable more of your consumers to become ambassadors by helping them share their experience with their own audiences?

- Can you create review points with your customers that reach long past the initial transaction and collect more evidence of connection?

- What stories of your customers or employees could you share with your audience to show connection?

- In what ways could you include more user-generated content in your communications?

- What could you create to educate your customers on why they should stay connected to you?

- How could you connect your audience with more content about their community as a whole, and not just your part in it?

9

Proving
Competence

SHORTLY AFTER I published *The Content Fuel Framework*, I got a phone call, out of the blue, from a publicist. He loved my book, he said, and wanted to help me with publicity. He promised that his company could get my book in front of *millions* of readers and generate *hundreds of thousands* of sales.

As a marketer myself, I was skeptical of his promise, particularly given the price point. It seemed far too good to be true, and I just couldn't see how this company could possibly get results like that. (Not ethically, anyway.)

I asked the representative on the phone if he could tell me about the tactics the company uses to get a book so much visibility with such a small budget. These were trade secrets, he said. He shared a few vague options—social media and other ads—but he more or less just assured me that the tactics were *very* effective.

I asked for the names of some of the authors the firm had worked with, thinking perhaps I had heard of one or two who could vouch for their process—witnesses. He said he wasn't able to name any of their authors due to NDAs, but assured me their authors were *very* successful. He told me the company did have a few testimonials on their site but admitted that the most recent one had been posted more than 10 years ago.

While the salesman continued his pitch, I opened my laptop to check out the company's online presence myself. I couldn't find any evidence of a Twitter account, but I did find a YouTube channel. It had only eight subscribers, and even the best-performing video hadn't reached 600 views. (To be clear, there's nothing inherently wrong with having eight subscribers or 600 views. We all have to start somewhere. But if you're telling me you can help me reach millions of people, I'd certainly expect a little bit more than that.)

When I typed the company's name into Google in search of more information, the top suggestions were to add "complaints" or to check out the Better Business Bureau. I didn't need to see their website to know that I wasn't interested.

By now you see what I'm doing here: in telling you this real-life story, I'm establishing proof about what I'm about to claim—specifically, that if you say you are excellent at what you do, you have to be able to back that up. In this case, I had given the company the benefit of the doubt at first. I know I've had amazing clients that I couldn't name due to NDAs, and I've also suffered from the "cobbler's children have no shoes" syndrome where my own online activity has taken a back seat to client priorities. But without any proof that this company was actually capable of doing anything they claimed, how could I possibly move forward in working with them?

It didn't help that this was a cold call. Skepticism about competence is particularly high with unknown brands, new companies, and products with which the consumer isn't familiar.

Types of Competence Claims

Claiming to be competent means insisting that you are capable of delivering on what's promised. Competence claims probably make up the largest number of business claims, if only because of the various ways that competence can be defined and analyzed. In varying contexts, "competence" could refer to expertise, knowledge, efficiency, experience, ability, capacity, performance, merit, skills, judgment, accuracy, attention to detail, and more. That said, these claims typically relate to the qualifications, reliability, or consistency of a company, product, service, or individual.

I've intentionally left claims about competence for last, because competence truly is the bare minimum that consumers expect. If you're not able to do good work, you shouldn't be in business (or you won't be for long). In a survey by PricewaterhouseCoopers, almost half of all consumers said they would abandon a brand if they felt that the employees were not knowledgeable.

Many competence claims cite **experience** or **legacy** as a differentiating factor, emphasizing that they are not new to the industry and have the right background to prepare them to provide top-notch products and services. Sometimes this is done with a direct reference to how long the company has been in business, and many companies have a sort of "implied claim" by including phrasing like "since 1935" or similar in their marketing materials.

Here are some real-world examples of competence claims related to experience:

> "Fluent in finance."—Barclays
>
> "The crown jewellers for 150 years."—Garrard
>
> "A century of global services."—Bank of China
>
> "Never stop. Never settle. Since 1765."—Hennessy

Other competence claims emphasize the **reliability** of a business's products or services, with a focus on consistency to help demonstrate that they will be there to deliver the expected quality for their clients, day in and day out. Here are some real-life examples of reliability and consistency claims:

> "Fresh checked every day."—Winn-Dixie
>
> "Can you hear me now? Good."—Verizon
>
> "Consistent low prices."—Wegmans
>
> "The reliable airline."—KLM Royal Dutch Airlines

Competence claims are also some of the easiest claims to prove, because competence is the foundation for many of the other claim types we've already discussed. As a result, much of the information that follows will echo back to the role these types of content can play in proving convenience, comparability, commitment, and connection.

Proving Competence with Corroboration

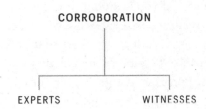

Corroboration—in the form of social proof is particularly compelling when it comes to proving competence, so even in instances when you are using experts or witnesses to prove other claims, the validity you are proving in regards to competence should also see a boost.

For example, Amy Landino's **expert corroboration** in the form of her video review of Adobe Spark helped show the tool's convenience, but it also served as proof that the product would deliver on what was promised. Subaru's list of awards successfully proved how well they compare to the competition, but also cataloged their proficiency in a variety of areas. Sharing awards and certifications related to causes and people you value helps corroborate your commitments and connections, but it also shows that you've successfully done the work needed to win recognition.

Similarly, any of the customer success stories you share to prove other claims will also help prove your competence through **witness corroboration**. If, in proving your comparability claims, you share a customer story that includes praise for how much better your solution worked, then your capabilities will already be on display. You can't be *better* than the competition if you aren't even *good* to begin with.

If proving competence is of particular importance—as may be the case if you're doing reparative work on your reputation—focusing on reviews is a great idea. Encourage satisfied customers to leave reviews that underscore how well you were able to address their challenges. Spend time replying to negative comments to offer clarity on the circumstances and to offer to fix any issues. (Check out *Hug Your Haters* by Jay Baer for more on how to handle these interactions in a way that makes both your professionalism and your competence shine.)

Proving Competence with Demonstration

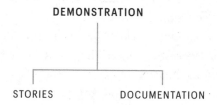

Sharing **success stories** is a great way to demonstrate your competence to your audience, particularly when they are told from your own perspective or that of your employees. In all customer success stories, you're likely identifying competence as an underpinning of whatever results were created.

But if you're focused specifically on competence, it can also be valuable to bring in benchmarks, expectations, and averages as a means of showing how your performance meets or exceeds those standards.

Ultimately, though, one of the best ways to prove competence is to provide **documentation** of that competence in action, allowing the audience to see your talent (and your team's talent) with their own eyes. This tends to work best for businesses with a physical product or an element of craftsmanship.

Food industry workers have mastered the art of creating engaging social video that demonstrates their impressive handiwork. Chefs demonstrate mesmerizing knife skills. Bakers show off unbelievably lifelike cake decorations. Street vendors and bartenders juggle and perform illusions as they prep customers' orders. Artists and builders have used time-lapse or accelerated video to show off their skills too. As we watch hours (or days) of masterful work compressed into 30 or 60 seconds, we can see all the talent of the process. With each stroke of a pen, drag of a paintbrush, swing of a hammer, or threading of a needle, these makers demonstrate their mastery of their craft for all to see.

TikTok has also given rise to a new breed of "cleanfluencers" who have earned their clout by showing off the transformations they create. Home cleaning services, car detailers, rug cleaners, and stuffed animal restorationists show their hands as they wash, scrub, and rinse their way through messes, revealing miraculous before-and-after comparisons. Each video provides further proof that these detail-oriented folks can't be stopped in their pursuit of pristineness.

Proving Competence with Education

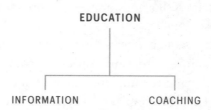

Educational content is particularly good for proving competence because the content's existence is contingent upon you having the knowledge and experience to be able to create it in the first place. Simply by offering educational content, you're proving to your audience that you know enough to provide value to them.

One way to provide educational content that proves competence is to **inform** your audience—for example, to focus on busting myths or dispelling common misconceptions about your product type or industry. This gives you the opportunity to provide your audience with accurate information to aid in decision-making.

Another fantastic way to prove your competence through education is to **coach** your audience through a process—you are showing your knowledge and experience instead of just declaring it. Plenty of brands have used instructional guides, tutorials, and courses as a way to wrap competence up in a helpful package. For example, food sustainability advocate and chef Max La Manna populates his Instagram feed with easy low-waste recipe videos, and he has authored a book of recipes that consumers can easily replicate at home. Starbucks' Coffee Academy offers a series of downloadable

Brew Guides that teach coffee aficionados how to use a Chemex brewer, how to make cold brew, and more. The search engine optimization tool Ahrefs offers courses that walk users through how to do keyword research and how to use that search data for their marketing.

Not only is this type of content helpful for prospects and consumers looking for guidance on how to successfully carry out a process, but it also serves as powerful evidence of the fact that you really know your stuff and can be trusted to assist with related processes that your audience may need your help with.

You can also both inform and coach your audience through thought leadership, where an individual representing an organization shares their opinions, thoughts, analysis, or other insights about their industry. This includes things like op-eds in local papers and magazines, LinkedIn essays, and blog posts about best practices or trends. When your leadership is willing and able to share what they know with prospects and customers, it can go a long way toward showing the depth of knowledge that lives within your organization. In fact, 59% of consumers believe thought leadership is more trustworthy when assessing the capabilities and competencies of an organization, compared to its marketing or product information.

Exactly What to Do Now

BY PHIL M JONES

Competence should be table stakes for every modern business. Yet in a world with so much transparency, the levels of competence can be really quite diverse. Proving how your competence shows up in this modern marketplace requires a little critical thinking. Apply effort and energy in strategically powerful areas and let the evidence, rather than the ego, do the talking.

Of course, competence needs to exist before evidence can support it. But assuming the competence is really there, get to work on building your plan with the answers to these questions:

- How could you start to insert review content into your marketing mix to prove your competence?

- What can you do to create a quantity of quality reviews that is high enough to be actually obnoxious? (Think at least five times as many as your comparable competitor.)

- How can you continue to communicate with your customers far past the transaction in order to create long-term success stories?

- What images could you create that show you doing what you say you do?

- Can you use your website and your knowledge to teach consumers about your industry as a whole and not just your place in it?

- What "how to" content can you create that shows people exactly how to do what you do (while demonstrating that they should probably just hire you to do it!)?

Conclusion
Are You Ready to Prove It?

MARKETERS, SALES PROFESSIONALS, and business owners have always faced challenges, from staffing and budgeting to competition and evolving markets. But in a digital economy where the competition is just a thumb-swipe away, differentiating yourself and winning over prospects must be your key priority. Still, earning the trust of prospects and maintaining the loyalty of customers is no easy feat. A study from the American Association of Advertising Agencies revealed that only 4% of consumers believe advertisers and marketers practice integrity.

Lucky for you—and your customers—you're now armed with all the information you need to identify the business claims you are making, and to build a body of evidence that supports each and every one. You now have the power to put your integrity on display and differentiate yourself in a way that can't be denied.

You, my friend, are a person who proves it.

You use content to corroborate your claims by providing sources who can act as social proof. You borrow the credibility of expert sources who lend their knowledge, and you use your customers as witnesses to the claims you make.

You use content to demonstrate the truth of your claims, so the audience can see it with their own eyes. You use stories to recount past examples of your fulfillment of those claims, and you document the truth of your claims as it's happening.

You use content to educate your audience so they can understand why your claims are both important and true. You inform them of the facts they need to make the best decisions, and you coach them through the processes that make your claims true.

Just as many court cases are years in the making, you won't compile and distribute all of your proof overnight. Winning over customers, building a relationship with them, and overcoming their skepticism is an ongoing process. If you're willing to put in the continued effort to provide proof of your claims, then you will be adopting a sustainable way to earn—and keep—the trust of the consumers who matter to you.

If you want your customers to truly know that you are who you say you are and you do what you say you do, you'll need to turn "providing proof" into a practice. Over time, you'll create an ever-growing body of work to back up every claim you are making.

As a person who proves it, you'll also be on the lookout for new claims that you make going forward. From routine social media posts referencing your products to new name tags that invite customers to "ask me anything," you'll now be able to easily spot any new claims that have popped up during your day-to-day operations and marketing as your business grows and evolves. And when new claims do appear in your customers' journey, you'll be prepared to devise a plan for proof that addresses every single one. Because any time you make a promise or set an expectation for your customers—or any time a prospect comes upon a claim for the first time—you can bet they're thinking, "I'll believe it when I see it."

Your audience is waiting for you to prove it. Now that you know how, don't make them wait too long.

Acknowledgments

THE AUTHORS would like to thank Phil's wife, Charlotte, and Melanie's husband, Yasin, who have both proven how important love and support are in creating anything of substance. We're eternally grateful for your encouragement and patience, not only throughout this project but for so many countless others.

We'd also like to thank the team at Page Two who helped transform an idea and a Google Doc into the finished product you see before you. You've proven to each of us time and again what a talented team you are, and we're grateful to have been able to work with you once again.

And we'd be remiss if we didn't thank our incredible executive assistants—Bonnie and Laura—who consistently prove the value of organization and helped make sure that all of the things that needed to happen for this book to come to life happened.

Melanie would like to thank the many coffee shops that provided Wi-Fi, beverages, and a place to focus while writing this book, especially NoRa Cafe in Raleigh, North Carolina.

Phil would like to express huge gratitude to the thousands of businesses he has been invited to consult, which repeatedly prompted the "How can we prove it?" question to be asked.

But above all else, the authors would like to bring attention to the process of collaboration and how this project itself is proof of the fact that the best way to produce anything is often to do it *together*.

Notes

For a clickable version of the list below, head to peoplewhoproveit.com.

Chapter 1: The Case for Evidence

p. 6   "what a company says or the actions it takes." "Consumers Find It Harder to Trust Companies—But Are They Being Hypocritical?" MarketingCharts, January 15, 2020, marketingcharts.com/brand-related/csr-111584.

p. 6   "more likely to be skeptical toward advertising." Carl Obermiller, Eric Spangenberg, and Douglas L. MacLachlan, "Ad Skepticism: The Consequences of Disbelief," *Journal of Advertising* 34, no. 3 (2005): 7–17, doi.org/10.1080/009133 67.2005.10639199.

p. 7   "incurred by the EU adult population over a two-year period." *Survey on "Scams and Fraud Experienced by Consumers": Final Report*, European Commission, January 2020, cc.europa.eu/info/sites/default/files/aid_development_ cooperation_fundamental_rights/ensuring_aid_ effectiveness/documents/survey_on_scams_and_fraud_ experienced_by_consumers_-_final_report.pdf.

p. 7   "more than $177 million to investment scams in 2021." "Scam Statistics, 2021," Scamwatch, Australian Competition & Consumer Commission, scamwatch.gov .au/scam-statistics?scamid=all&date=2021.

p. 7 "from online shopping scams specifically." "New Data Shows FTC Received 2.2 Million Fraud Reports from Consumers in 2020," News & Events, Federal Trade Commission, February 4, 2021, ftc.gov/news-events/press-releases/2021/02/new-data-shows-ftc-received-2-2-million-fraud-reports-consumers.

p. 10 "before judging them either credible or unreliable." David Lewis and Darren Bridger, *The Soul of the New Consumer: Authenticity—What We Buy and Why in the New Economy* (Boston: Nicholas Brealey, 2001).

p. 10 "you must have at least that level of support." *Advertising and Marketing on the Internet: Rules of the Road*, Federal Trade Commission, September 2000, ftc.gov/system/files/documents/plain-language/bus28-advertising-and-marketing-internet-rules-road2018.pdf. Emphasis in original.

p. 10 "the accuracy of factual claims they have made." Directive 2006/114/EC of the European Parliament and of the Council of 12 December 2006 Concerning Misleading and Comparative Advertising, EUR-Lex, eur-lex.europa.eu/legal-content/EN/TXT/?uri=celex%3A32006L0114.

Chapter 2: How Trust Works

p. 13 "can be relied upon to deliver on its promises." Deepak Sirdeshmukh, Jagdip Singh, and Barry Sabol, "Consumer Trust, Value, and Loyalty in Relational Exchanges" (working paper, Marketing Science Institute Report No. 01-116, 2001), msi.org/wp-content/uploads/2020/06/MSI_Report_01-116.pdf.

p. 15 "to drive profitable customer action." "What Is Content Marketing?" Content Marketing Institute, contentmarketinginstitute.com/what-is-content-marketing.

Chapter 3: The Five Claim Types

p. 20 "with the highest level of integrity." "Welcome to American Express," About, American Express, about.americanexpress.com/home/default.aspx#mission.

p. 21   "when they choose a retailer." Alex Jewell, "How Convenience Is Now Key in Purchasing Decisions, According to
the Latest Consumer Research from Linnworks," *Retail
Gazette*, March 31, 2021, retailgazette.co.uk/blog/2021/03/
how-convenience-is-now-key-in-purchasing-decisions
-according-to-the-latest-consumer-research-from-linnworks.

p. 21   "and 51% check out four or more sites." Lauren Freedman,
Comparison Shopping Is a Way of Life, E-Tailing Group,
September 2009, e-tailing.com/content/wp-content/
uploads/2009/12/winbuyer_102209_brief.pdf.

p. 22   "speak out on issues they care about." *Consumer Culture
Report*, 5W Public Relations, 2020, 5wpr.com/new/
research/consumer-culture-report.

p. 22   "whether that's in a brick-and-mortar shop or online." "Consumers Welcome Personalized Offerings but Businesses
Are Struggling to Deliver, Finds Accenture Interactive
Personalization Research," Accenture, October 13, 2016,
newsroom.accenture.com/news/consumers-welcome
-personalized-offerings-but-businesses-are-struggling-to
-deliver-finds-accenture-interactive-personalization
-research.htm.

p. 23   "to deliver good-quality products or services." "Brand Trust
Is Becoming More Important: Here Are Some Key Stats and
Themes," MarketingCharts, July 10, 2019, marketingcharts
.com/brand-related/brand-loyalty-109127.

p. 27   "called the product out if the claims were false." Gary T.
Ford, Darlene B. Smith, and John L. Swasy, "Consumer
Skepticism of Advertising Claims: Testing Hypotheses from
Economics of Information," *Journal of Consumer Research*
16, no. 4 (March 1990): 433–441, dx.doi.org/10.1086/
209228.

Chapter 4: Building a Body of Evidence

p. 30   "and ability to attract talent." "Methodology for World's
Most Admired Companies," *Fortune*, 2017, fortune.com/
worlds-most-admired-companies/2017/methodology.

p. 31   "non-winning companies on a number of key metrics."
Kevin B. Hendricks and Vinod R. Singhal, "Don't Count
TQM Out," *Quality Progress*, April 1999, 35–42, quality
-texas.org/wp-content/uploads/2014/11/Awards-and
-Organizational-Success-2.pdf. See figure 2 (page 38)
especially.

p. 32   "credible sources of information about a company." *Edelman
Trust Barometer 2021*, Edelman, 2021, edelman.com/sites/
g/files/aatuss191/files/2021-03/2021%20Edelman%20
Trust%20Barometer.pdf.

p. 32   "influencers' opinions more than any other source." Dina
Gerdeman, "Lipstick Tips: How Influencers Are Making
Over Beauty Marketing," Working Knowledge, Harvard
Business School, August 26, 2019, hbswk.hbs.edu/item/
lipstick-tips-how-influencers-are-making-over-beauty
-marketing.

p. 33   "when it gets good ratings and reviews." As cited in "Brand
Trust Is Becoming More Important," MarketingCharts.

p. 33   "after the start of the pandemic in 2020." Rosie Murphy,
"Local Consumer Review Survey 2020," BrightLocal,
December 9, 2020, brightlocal.com/research/local
-consumer-review-survey-2020.

p. 33   "to validate the claims businesses make." Obermiller et al.,
"Ad Skepticism."

p. 33   "of a product with zero reviews." Georgios Askalidis and
Edward C. Malthouse, "The Value of Online Customer
Reviews," *RecSys: '16: Proceedings of the 10th ACM
Conference on Recommender Systems*, Association for
Computing Machinery, September 2016, 155–158, doi.org/
10.1145/2959100.2959181.

p. 33   "which means more customers can find them." Emily
Cullinan, "How to Use Customer Testimonials to Generate
62% More Revenue from Every Customer, Every Visit," Big
Commerce, bigcommerce.com/blog/customer-testimonial.

p. 33   "a revenue increase of between 5% and 9%." Michael
Blanding, "The Yelp Factor: Are Consumer Reviews Good
for Business?" Working Knowledge, Harvard Business

School, October 24, 2011, hbswk.hbs.edu/item/the-yelp
-factor-are-consumer-reviews-good-for-business.

p. 34   "highest performing brands stand out in the crowd."
"J.D. Power Syndicated Benchmark Awards," J.D. Power,
jdpower.com/business/awards.

p. 35   "helped someone similar to them." "Testimonials Statistics
2020," Wyzowl, wyzowl.com/testimonials-statistics.

p. 36   "coming in right behind tutorials." *Explore Instagram Video:
How to Convert, Engage, and Get More Followers with
Video*, Wibbitz, wibbitz.com/reports/instagram-followers
-video-report.

p. 37   "and increases their loyalty." *The Deloitte Consumer Review:
The Growing Power of Consumers*, Deloitte, 2014, www2
.deloitte.com/content/dam/Deloitte/uk/Documents/
consumer-business/consumer-review-8-the-growing
-power-of-consumers.pdf.

p. 37   "after consuming educational content." Charity Stebbins,
"Educational Content Makes Consumers 131% More
Likely to Buy," Conductor, July 6, 2017, conductor.com/
blog/2017/07/winning-customers-educational-content.

p. 38   "educate them about product features and benefits."
*The Truth About Online Consumers: 2017 Global Online
Consumer Report*, KPMG, 2017, assets.kpmg.com/content/
dam/kpmg/xx/pdf/2017/01/the-truth-about-online
-consumers.pdf.

p. 39   "more than videos about music or gaming." Chris Moore-
Broyles and LaToya Moore-Broyles, "Grabbing Consumer
Attention Is Hard. 'How-To' Content Can Help," Think with
Google, August 2018, thinkwithgoogle.com/marketing
-strategies/video/how-to-content.

Chapter 5: Proving Convenience

p. 47   "choose a retailer based on convenience." "Consumer View
Winter 2020," National Retail Federation, January 14, 2020,
nrf.com/research/consumer-view-winter-2020.

p. 49   "complicated or lengthy checkout process." "46 Cart
Abandonment Rate Statistics," Baymard Institute,

updated November 19, 2021, baymard.com/lists/cart
-abandonment-rate.

p. 49   "in their choice of online retailer." Jewell, "How Convenience
Is Now Key."

p. 53   "according to the National Retail Federation." "Consumer
View Winter 2020," National Retail Federation.

p. 54   "use their solution to power some or all of their payments."
The Visa Blog, all-lb.visa.com/visa-everywhere/blog.html.

Chapter 6: Proving Comparability

p. 63   "at least 16 minutes on comparing their options." Freedman,
Comparison Shopping Is a Way of Life.

p. 65   "are still on the road today." "Industry Reviews & Awards,"
Subaru, subaru.com/why-subaru/reviews-awards/
subaru.html.

p. 69   "a retailer who shows competitors' prices." Freedman,
Comparison Shopping Is a Way of Life.

Chapter 7: Proving Commitment

p. 77   "trust more companies with their data." "Four Steps
to Gaining Consumer Trust in Your Tech," Tech Effect,
PwC, pwc.com/us/en/tech-effect/cybersecurity/trusted
-tech.html.

p. 78   "from brands that align with their values." Gabrielle
Pickard-Whitehead, "71% of Consumers Prefer Buying
from Companies Aligned With Their Values," *Small
Business Trends*, February 19, 2020, smallbiztrends.com/
2020/02/brand-values-alignment.html.

p. 78   "to reduce their environmental impact." "Brand Trust Is
Becoming More Important," MarketingCharts.

p. 79   "and not just 'cause-exploitative.'" Marhana M. Anuar,
Khatijah Omar, and Osman Mohamad, "Does Skepticism
Influence Consumers Intention to Purchase Cause-Related
Products?" *International Journal of Business and Social
Science* 4, no. 5 (May 2013): 94–98, ijbssnet.com/journals/
Vol_4_No_5_May_2013/9.pdf.

p. 79   "easily accessible evidence to support its claim." "Screening
          of Websites for 'Greenwashing': Half of Green Claims Lack
          Evidence," Press Corner, European Commission, January
          28, 2021, ec.europa.eu/commission/presscorner/detail/en/
          ip_21_269.

p. 80   "highest standards of data privacy and security."
          Anupam Narula, Frank Milano, and Raj Singhal, "Building
          Consumer Trust: Protecting Personal Data in the Consumer
          Product Industry," Deloitte Insights, Deloitte, November
          14, 2014, www2.deloitte.com/us/en/insights/topics/risk
          -management/consumer-data-privacy-strategies.html.

p. 84   "such an evaluation in the first place." As cited in Alison
          Omens, "Of the 890 Largest US Companies, Only 65 Have
          Reviewed Their Gender Pay Gap and Made the Reports
          Public—And That Lack of Transparency Is Holding Women
          Back," *Business Insider*, April 2, 2019, businessinsider.com/
          us-public-companies-fail-to-release-pay-equity-reports
          -2019-4.

p. 86   "how harvesting palm oil contributes to deforestation."
          Looking Further with Ford: 2020 Trends, Ford Motor
          Company, 2019, media.ford.com/content/dam/
          fordmedia/North%20America/US/2019/12/11/2020
          -Ford-Trends.pdf.

p. 86   "read the privacy protection policy." Narula et al., "Building
          Consumer Trust."

p. 87   "I wanted to do something about it. But what?" Blake
          Mycoskie, "How I Did It: The TOMS Story," *Entrepreneur*,
          September 20, 2011, entrepreneur.com/article/220350.

p. 87   "own narrative can be particularly effective." *Edelman Trust
          Barometer 2021*.

p. 88   "would also increase their trust." Narula et al., "Building
          Consumer Trust."

Chapter 8: Proving Connection

p. 94   "a chatbot or some other automated process." Tom
          Puthiyamadam and José Reyes, *Experience Is Everything:*

Here's How to Get It Right, PwC, 2018, pwc.com/us/en/zz
-test/assets/pwc-consumer-intelligence-series-customer
-experience.pdf.

p. 96   "more trusting of scientists than any other source." *Edelman
Trust Barometer 2021.*

p. 97   "ask customers to review a purchase." *From Reviews to
Revenue, Volume 1: How Star Ratings and Review Content
Influence Purchase*, PowerReviews and Northwestern
University, 2016, powerreviews.com/wp-content/uploads/
2019/02/From-Reviews-to-Revenue-Northwestern-Report
-Volume-1.pdf.

p. 101   "reason for shopping small is to keep money local." "Buying
Local Statistics for 2021: Survey Finds 70% of Americans
Shop Small," MintLife, Intuit, January 11, 2021, mint.intuit
.com/blog/money-etiquette/buying-local-statistics-survey.

p. 102   "for their classrooms, without getting reimbursed." Gail
O'Connor, "The School-Supply Gap," *One Day*, Teach
for America, September 8, 2019, teachforamerica.org/
one-day/top-issues/the-school-supply-gap; Grace Sparks,
"94% of Teachers Spend Their Own Money on School
Supplies," CNN, May 22, 2018, cnn.com/ampstories/us/
teachers-spend-own-money-on-school-supplies.

Chapter 9: Proving Competence

p. 109   "the employees were not knowledgeable." Puthiyamadam
and Reyes, *Experience Is Everything.*

p. 115   "its marketing or product information." *2020 B2B Thought
Leadership Impact Study*, Edelman Business Marketing
and LinkedIn, November 14, 2019, edelman.com/
research/2020-b2b-thought-leadership-impact-study.

Conclusion: Are You Ready to Prove It?

p. 119   "believe advertisers and marketers practice integrity."
Maureen Morrison, "No One Trusts Advertising or Media
(Except Fox News)," *Ad Age*, April 24, 2015, adage.com/
article/media/marketers-media-trusts/298221.

About the Authors

Melanie Deziel

Melanie Deziel is a speaker, award-winning content creator, and lifelong storyteller on a mission to share the power of compelling and credible content with others. She is the author of the bestselling marketing and business communications book *The Content Fuel Framework: How to Generate Unlimited Story Ideas*, and co-founder of The Convoy, a B2B marketplace that pools the buying power of independently owned businesses to help negotiate discounts on everyday tools and services.

When she's not leading marketing efforts for The Convoy, Melanie gives keynotes, leads workshops, and appears on both TV and podcasts to teach businesses and marketing professionals how to create better content. As the first editor of branded content at *The New York Times*' T Brand Studio, Melanie wrote the sponsored content pieces that won the 2014 and 2015 Best Native Advertising Execution

OMMA Awards, including the acclaimed "Women Inmates" piece for Netflix. She was a founding member of HuffPost Partner Studio, and she served as director of creative strategy at Time Inc., building branded content strategy across 35+ US media properties, including *Time, Fortune, People, Sports Illustrated,* and *Entertainment Weekly.*

In the world of academia, Melanie developed and taught a graduate course on content marketing for Fairleigh Dickinson University, and she also designed and taught a graduate course based on *The Content Fuel Framework* for the City University of New York. She has worked as an adjunct professor for Syracuse University's Newhouse School of Public Communications, teaching graduate courses in digital marketing, social media, and more.

Witness Melanie "Prove It" at storyfuel.co.

Phil M Jones

Phil M Jones is a master of influence and persuasion. He is the author of multiple bestselling business books (as well as one children's book) and the producer of "the most listened to" non-fiction audiobook of all time.

Entering the world of business at the age of 14 with nothing more than a bucket and sponge, Phil went from washing cars on weekends solo to hiring a fleet of car-washers, resulting in him earning more than his teachers by the time he was 15. By his early 20s he was leading teams of experienced sales professionals while guiding Premier League football clubs to maximize their sponsorships and licensing agreements, and helping to grow an independent real estate business to revenues in excess of $240 million.

In 2008, Phil started his training and consulting business from scratch, and has since grown a deep body of work that showcases his core belief that changing your words can truly change your world. Today, he is known for his best-selling book *Exactly What to Say: The Magic Words for Influence and Impact* and for the thought leadership he has delivered as a speaker and advisor to 800 industries across 59 countries and five continents. Phil was the youngest-ever winner of the British Excellence in Sales and Marketing Award and is one of fewer than 200 living members of the National Speakers Association Hall of Fame. As president of the market-leading communications agency Orange & Gray, he is also a strategic advisor to pioneering leaders of the world's biggest brands.

Witness Phil "Prove It" at philmjones.com.

Additional Tools for Trust

The Content Fuel Framework

Want to prove it but stuck on how to build evidence for your claims with brand-aligned, consistent stories? Melanie Deziel's *The Content Fuel Framework* is an adaptable and evergreen guide to generating unlimited story ideas for marketers and creators.

Never before have we consumed as much content, in as many forms, and in as many places as we do now. This means marketers, creators, and anyone who communicates with an audience is under more pressure than ever to deliver unique content, consistently. How can you fill all those web pages, social feeds, blogs, and newsletters, every single day?

The Content Fuel Framework shows you how to maximize your creativity by systematizing it, making idea generation effortless and nearly automatic. No more writer's block. No more asking "what should I post?" No more waiting for that "big idea" to show up in its own time. *The Content Fuel Framework* will challenge you—and enable you—to tell stories in entirely new ways.

Head to **storyfuel.co** to add this title to your toolkit.

"A simple, yet highly effective approach to inspire numerous rich ideas. This method will rescue any content marketing program—a savior."

LEE ODDEN, CEO and co-founder, TopRank Marketing

Exactly What to Say

The success or failure of almost every interaction is affected by the ability to choose the right words at the right time. Hard work, talent, and perfect timing can all have a great impact on your success—but without the ability to steer a conversation and create an agreeable outcome, your effort can be wasted. If you've ever found yourself lost for words, or have come away from a conversation without the result you are looking for, then what you need is *Exactly What to Say*.

Learn the Magic Words you need to know to establish that crucial trust connection—and get what more of you want. Phil M Jones's international bestseller will provide you with the skills you need to increase your confidence in conversation, and boost your success in all your endeavors.

Head to **philmjones.com** to add this guide to your trust arsenal.

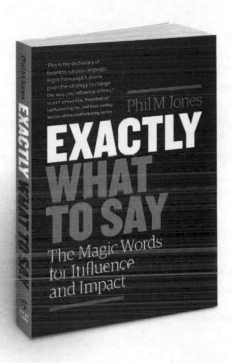

"This is the dictionary of business success language. Right from page 1, you're given the strategy to change the way you influence others."

SCOTT STRATTEN, president, UnMarketing Inc.; bestselling author of the UnMarketing series

As you build your case and compile evidence that proves all of your business claims, head to **peoplewhoproveit.com** for additional resources.